I0796566

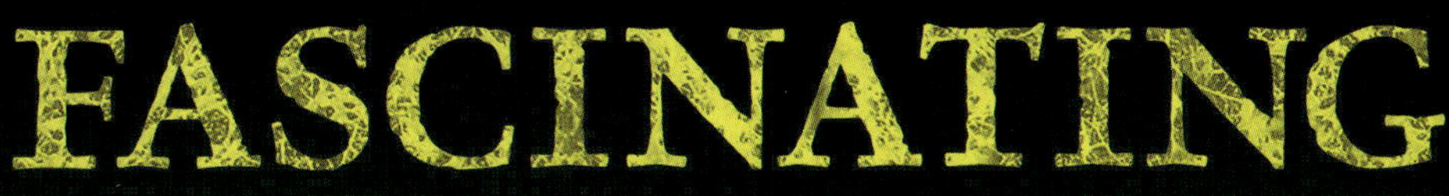

FASCINATING FUNGI

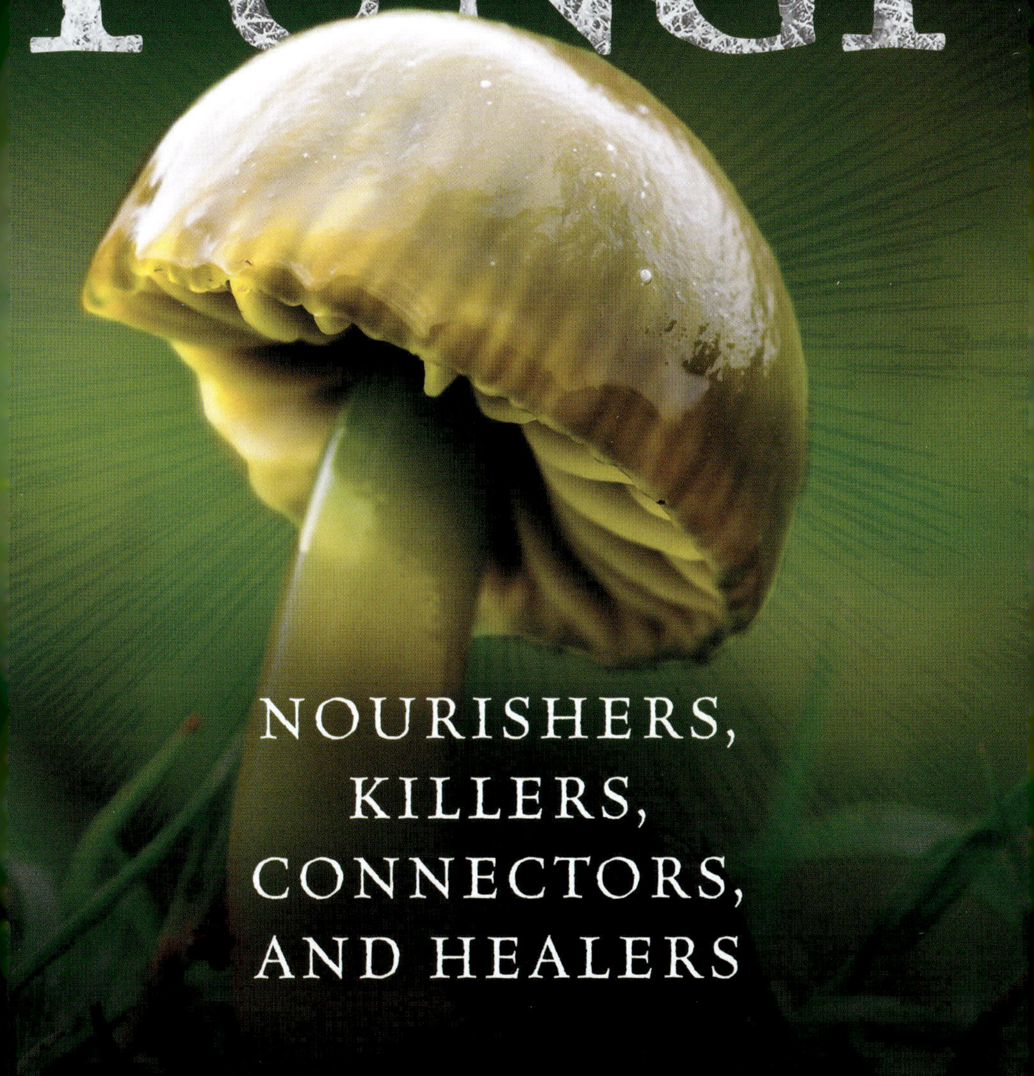

NOURISHERS, KILLERS, CONNECTORS, AND HEALERS

Karen Latchana Kenney

TF CB

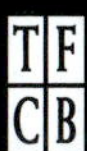

TWENTY-FIRST CENTURY BOOKS / MINNEAPOLIS

To my uncle Chris, a real lad of the Irish woods and fellow fungi fan

Twenty-First Century Books™
An imprint of Lerner Publishing Group, Inc.
241 First Avenue North
Minneapolis, MN 55401 USA

For reading levels and more information, look up this title at www.lernerbooks.com.

Main body text set in Univers LT Std.
Typeface provided by Adobe Systems.
Map and diagrams by Laura K. Westlund on pp. 66, 76, 103, 106.

Library of Congress Cataloging-in-Publication Data

Names: Kenney, Karen Latchana, author.
Title: Fascinating fungi : nourishers, killers, connectors, and healers / Karen Latchana Kenney.
Description: Minneapolis : Twenty-First Century Books , [2025] | Includes bibliographical references and index. | Audience: Ages 12–18 | Audience: Grades 7–9 | Summary: "From helping bread rise to capturing pollutants, fungi can do many incredible and even unexpected things. Explore the world of fungi, including strange sights, medicine, underground webs, and more"— Provided by publisher.
Identifiers: LCCN 2024017632 (print) | LCCN 2024017633 (ebook) | ISBN 9798765611173 (lib. bdg.) | ISBN 9798765619346 (epub)
Subjects: LCSH: Fungi—Juvenile literature. | BISAC: YOUNG ADULT NONFICTION / Science & Nature / Biology
Classification: LCC QK603.5 .K46 2025 (print) | LCC QK603.5 (ebook) | DDC 579.5—dc23/eng/20240624

LC record available at https://lccn.loc.gov/2024017632
LC ebook record available at https://lccn.loc.gov/2024017633

Manufactured in the United States of America
2-1013963-51744-2/19/2026

TABLE OF CONTENTS

THE YEW THAT WASN'T AND OTHER HUMONGOUS THINGS

In a world where forests didn't even exist, carbon dioxide filled the air, and mosslike plants blanketed the land, fungi were already doing unexpected things. It was four hundred million years ago during the early Devonian period, and Earth's life was primitive and experimental. While trilobites, simple corals, and giant armored fish were some of the creatures teeming in the vast oceans where all life began, not much had ventured out except for simple organisms. The ancestors of mosslike plants had been some of the first life to escape. And only wingless insects burrowed in that world above the water. But Earth was beginning to green, setting the conditions for life on land to bloom with complex organisms.

Rocky, fossilized clues write the story of this time. One clue found in the 1840s was especially unusual . . . shocking even—a fossilized alien form that may have towered above the ground and all life on it. It's possible it was the tallest living thing on land during the Devonian period, and it didn't quite make sense to scientists who studied it. The person who found the specimen in question was geoscientist William Logan, who was doing a geological survey of Canada's vast wilderness in the summer of 1843 near Gaspé Bay in Quebec, Canada. In 1855 Logan gave his collection of findings to John William Dawson, a Canadian geologist known for his work studying fossilized plants.

Dawson looked through the collection and was especially interested in one specimen, which resembled wood but was from a time before trees were believed to have existed. When he studied microscopic slices of the specimen, he saw loose tissue and a mesh of threads. Intrigued, he visited the original site and found more of these fossils trapped in the sandstone and shale. After further study, Dawson had a theory. He thought this ancient flora could be the rotted wood of a coniferous tree with a fungus aiding in its demise—that would help explain the fossil's simple and disorganized composition, which lacked rings and grains typical of fossilized wood. Yet the differences were apparent. Some of its tissue seemed pastelike, and no evidence of leaves or fruiting bodies were found. Dawson even wrote in his notes that what he saw was "like mycelium of fungus." Despite the incomplete match, Dawson determined it was an ancient yew tree and named it *Prototaxites*, meaning "first yew." He was convinced it was one of the first trees, and nearby sites surfaced large loglike samples, some 2 to 3 feet (0.6 to 0.9 m) in diameter, which only strengthened his belief.

The name *Prototaxites* stuck, but Dawson's determination that it was one of the first trees didn't sit well with everyone in the scientific community. In 1872 British botanist William

Carruthers, who had studied Dawson's samples, publicly denied Dawson's claims. Carruthers said there was no way this was a conifer tree. Instead, he proposed it was likely an algae, although it might possibly be a fungus or lichen. Over time, scientific opinion shifted, and *Prototaxites* was widely thought to be a distant relative of kelp, despite strong evidence that it grew on land.

For the next one hundred or so years, *Prototaxites* remained a debated mystery, until paleobotanist Francis Hueber, from the Smithsonian National Museum of Natural History, became interested in finding the answer. He meticulously studied Dawson's notes and traveled to Canada, Saudi Arabia, and Australia to collect more similar samples. For twenty years, he examined the inner structure of the ancient species, compared it with modern fungi, and saw that the similarities seemed undeniable. In 2001 Hueber published his findings. *Prototaxites* was not an ancient yew tree and not an algae either—it was likely a gigantic extinct fungus, one that reached heights of over 20 feet (6 m) tall.

Although not everyone agreed with his beliefs, Dawson published a treelike reconstruction of *Prototaxites* in 1888.

THE DEBATE CONTINUES

Science is always changing and evolving, and as Dawson's theory was challenged, so is Hueber's. A theory is a best guess based on the evidence known at the time. Since Hueber declared *Prototaxites* a fungus, other scientists have challenged this theory. His remains the most widely accepted, but other scientists have proposed *Prototaxites* could have been a lichen or an extinct lineage of fungus, one unlike the fungi we find today. Another idea is that it was a fungus that may have grown horizontally, instead of vertically as Hueber describes.

ANOTHER HUMONGOUS FUNGUS

While Hueber was completing his study of the ancient fungus, a modern-day discovery changed scientists' understanding of fungi too. Before 1998 the largest organism thought to exist on Earth was the blue whale, a behemoth of an ocean mammal that grows up to 110 feet (33.5 m) long and can weigh more than 165 tons (150 t). Yet the discovery of an organism in the Blue Mountains of Oregon shattered that idea. The organism lived mostly underground, beneath a forest of conifer trees, and remained undetected for thousands of years . . . as it grew and grew and grew.

Some call it a forest destroyer. It leaves behind mere skeletons of trees. That's what workers at the Malheur National Forest in eastern Oregon saw in 1998—large areas of conifer trees were dying. When they confirmed the presence of *Armillaria ostoyae* (commonly called the shoestring, or honey, fungus), they invited scientists to come in and study it. Growing along tree roots, the fungus's threadlike hyphae exude digestive enzymes, which slowly eat away the roots as the fungus spreads in a white film under the tree's bark, cutting off nutrients and water, and eventually killing the entire tree.

Forestry scientists accepted the invitation and came in to study the fungus, digging out samples from across thousands of acres of the forest. The results were unbelievable. Not only were the samples within the 3.5 square mile (9 sq. km) radius all the same kind of fungus, but they were also from the same individual organism. DNA analysis identified the species, and a type of self-recognition test to identify individuals proved it. Based on the area it covered, scientists estimated its weight at up to 35,000 tons (31,751 t)—equal to more than two hundred blue whales. And knowing its growth rate, scientists think the fungus may be up to 8,650 years old. At this size, the fungus is one of the largest-known organisms on the planet—larger than any dinosaur that existed before it—and so scientists aptly named it the Humongous Fungus. But nobody knows; maybe even larger fungi could be quietly growing beneath our feet.

HIDDEN WEBS, MYSTERIOUS MUSHROOMS

From ancient giants to underground titans, what's most clear about fungi is how little we know about them. Just dig down a bit in the ground and you'll see their webs gripping the soil, clinging to roots, and sprouting what we see aboveground—mushrooms. These mushrooms are what we know best about fungi, even though they're minute compared to their parent mycelium. They appear suddenly, the most visible part of this mostly invisible being, and disappear just as quickly after ensuring new fungi will spread.

These mushrooms are just the fungi we can easily see

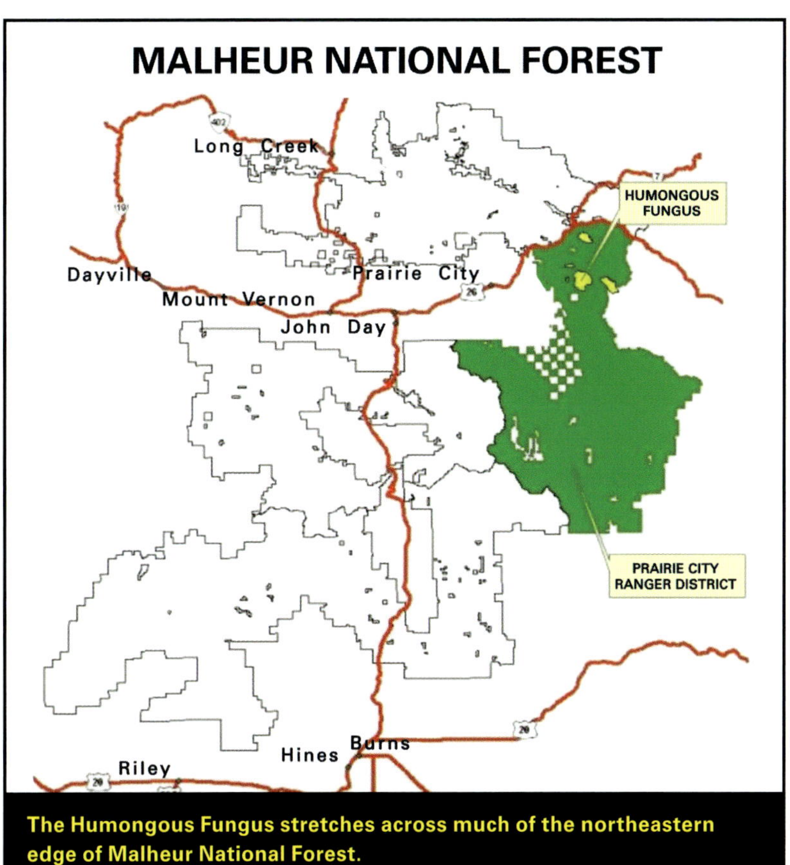

The Humongous Fungus stretches across much of the northeastern edge of Malheur National Forest.

in nature—in forests, in our gardens, and growing along with our food. But fungi are almost everywhere—from the environment around you to inside your own body, shaping how you and other animals live, affecting how life on Earth develops and grows, and even helping the planet heal. With incredible powers, many yet to be understood, fungi are the ultimate life connectors. Fungi can nourish or poison us, heal us miraculously or kill us mercilessly, and alter our perceptions or heal our trauma. They can feed plants symbiotically or, like the Humongous Fungus, decimate entire forests, and they once ruled the land, helping to make conditions just right for other organisms to appear.

Fungi can survive just about anywhere too. From frozen, barren landscapes to hot, dry deserts, from inside plant tissue to inside our guts, from deep in the sea to the tops of the trees, and from toxic waste sites to zombified hosts—fungi know how to thrive.

Not quite plant and not quite animal, fungi are their own prolific thing. And a world of them is waiting—we just have to find them. Somewhere between 2.2 and 12 million fungi species are thought to exist, and since we've only found around 150,000 kinds, the majority are yet to be discovered. What can we learn from this uniquely strange and humble organism, mostly hidden from our sight? Every year we find more. Each day we learn more. We are just beginning to uncover the fascinating world of fungi and how they change the world.

CHAPTER 1

THE FUNGAL FAMILY

If you asked someone back in the 1950s what kind of organism fungi are, they likely would have said plants. Fungi grow in soil and have rigid cell walls like a plant. They have rootlike structures that absorb nutrients. They also have fruiting bodies—their mushrooms—which is how they reproduce with spores, a bit like pollen. And fungi are immobile, staying put just like plants.

Yet there are some huge differences between fungi and plants. Fungi can grow in complete darkness and don't need sunlight to manufacture their food. But, according to an older classification system, all organisms fell into just two kingdoms: animal or plant. So, for a few centuries (and despite their clear differences), fungi seemed much more suited to being classified as part of the plant world.

This first classification system originated in the 1700s, when scientists had fewer tools to study organisms. Mushrooms were believed to be primitive plants in the two-kingdom system. With DNA sequencing and other scientific advancements in the twentieth century, scientists could more closely study life on Earth. So, the two-hundred-year-old classification system evolved, and in 1957 American ecologist Robert Whittaker proposed a major change. His innovative system used two main criteria for classification: mode of nutrition and how cells are organized. In 1969 he concluded that life existed in five kingdoms: monera (bacteria, single-cell organisms without a nucleus), protista (algae, single-cell organisms with

Robert Whittaker's classification system broke life down into five kingdoms. Some modern scientists still use these five, but most split monera into two separate kingdoms: bacteria and archaea.

a nucleus), fungi (mushrooms and mycelium, yeasts, and molds—multicelled organisms with chitin in their cell walls that digest food outside their bodies), plantae (plants, multicelled organisms that produce their own food), and animalia (animals, multicelled organisms that digest food inside their bodies).

Finally, fungi ruled their own kingdom—not quite animal and not quite plant, but existing somewhere in between. This kingdom is made of eukaryotic organisms (ones with membranous cells that contain a nucleus), including yeast, molds, lichen, and filamentous fungi that produce mushrooms.

EVOLUTION OF FUNGI

While fungi share some characteristics with plants, they share quite a few characteristics with animals too. Like animals, they do not produce oxygen but absorb it from outside of their bodies. They also consume food and release waste into their surroundings.

So, is it surprising that fungi are more closely related to animals than they are to plants? In the early 1990s, scientists studied the DNA of modern species to understand their genetic relationships. As life evolved on Earth, species split off from common ancestors to develop separately. Plants, animals, and fungi once had a common ancestor. After plants split, fungi and humans still shared a common ancestor about 1.5 billion years ago. That means we have more in common with fungi than plants do!

As life on Earth developed, single-celled fungi moved from the water onto land, shedding their flagella (whiplike tails that propelled them in the water) and evolving into multicellular organisms. They slowly ate away at the rock on land, digesting minerals and nutrients and adding them to

MYCOLOGICAL SOCIETIES

Many people love learning about mushrooms, whether they're scientists or not. Mycological societies are organizations made for mushroom admirers, citizen and professional scientists, and foodies. For a small membership fee, anyone can join a mycological society and gain access to educational seminars with mycologists, group forays to hunt mushrooms, cooking demonstrations, and much more. Many states have their own societies, and the North American Mycological Association serves as a national organization for the United States, Canada, and Mexico.

The Minnesota Mycological Society was one of the first of these societies in the United States. Dr. Mary Whetstone founded it in 1898, a time when mycological scientific research and accurate information about fungi (then still grouped with plants) was scarce. As just the second woman in Minneapolis to be a physician, she helped found a charity hospital for women and children where she worked with many patients experiencing poverty and malnutrition. According to Peter Martignacco, president of the society, "Whetstone wanted to provide alternative nutrition for women and children suffering from poverty, and saw foraging as an opportunity for them to alleviate some of their hunger."

Whetstone's desire to help her patients drew her to mycology,

soil across the planet. Fungi also formed critical partnerships with algae, aquatic organisms that can photosynthesize, as algae spread onto dry land. The algae gave the fungi sugars from photosynthesis, and the fungi gave the algae water and minerals from the land. As the algae evolved and became multicellular organisms, they grew fleshy organs over their fungal partners' mycelium. Together, these evolved into the first roots of the plants they became. Plants grew larger and more diverse as they spread across the land. By nourishing the soil and partnering with algae, fungi drove the evolution of plant life, allowing early plants to flourish and develop into vast forests as she knew mushrooms were a nutritious food source. She worked with well-known mycologists around the country to identify species in Minnesota. Through the society's work, people in Minnesota learned more about which mushrooms in the state were safe to eat or poisonous, and local interest in mycology grew. In fact, one of the society's members, L. F. Lambert, developed the first pure culture mushroom spawn in the United States. It was used to reliably grow a single strain of mushroom. The spawn company he started in 1919 is still in operation.

The society has grown tremendously and had fourteen hundred members as of 2024. Over the last twenty years, the society has educated more than six thousand members on mushroom identification. The members meet regularly to share fungal findings, hear about research or issues, venture out on forays together, and even sponsor student research with scholarships. Members mentor and teach one another about the fungi they find in the state. They also collaborate with other societies and partner with government poison control centers. Some members stay on call with poison control centers to help identify poisonous mushrooms when needed, and through this collaboration, they have saved people's lives. Completely volunteer-run, this society is a vital source of grassroots education and enjoyment for the community.

that created the oxygenated atmosphere in which humans and other animals can thrive.

LIVING FUNGI

Fungi not only helped forests and ecosystems develop, but they also keep those systems healthy. Imagine a world with a thick layer of dead leaves, fallen trees, and dead animals covering the ground. Without fungi and bacteria, that is the world we would live in—one where nothing ever decomposed into the soil, a land littered with thick debris. Fungi do much of this difficult

A BILLION YEARS OLD?

It's rare to find fungal fossils that we can study. Most that are found are microscopic, too tiny to tell much from them. But in 2019 scientists reported finding something in the Canadian Arctic. It was trapped in shale, which possibly made up the bottom of an ancient estuary. These fossils were small too—about 0.0039 inches (0.1 mm) long—but just big enough to analyze. They had tiny bulbous structures with branching filaments attached. The team of scientists also studied the chemical composition of the microfossils using spectroscopy, seeing how the fossils' matter interacted with electromagnetic radiation. They found it reacted like chitin. The scientists determined that the fossils' shape along with the presence of chitin made them the earliest fungi ever found. By looking at the ratio of radioactive elements in the rock where the fossil was found, they estimated the fungi were around a billion years old—more than five hundred million years older than the fungi previously thought to be the oldest. Compare that to modern humans, who've been around for a mere three hundred thousand years.

work, reaching up from under forest floors to turn dead matter into food for the living and clearing the land for new plants and animals to occupy.

Not all fungi live under forests, but they all begin life as tiny spores. These are the reproductive cells of fungi, dispersed by their fruiting bodies. These small, lightweight spores move through the air, water, or inside animals to find a moist place with oxygen and the right food needed to germinate. If they do find a good place, the spores will begin growing hyphae—slender, cylindrical cells with rigid walls that contain chitin and glucan. The chitin, which is also found in arthropod exoskeletons, strengthens fungi and protects them from predators. Inside each cell are specialized organelles including a nucleus containing DNA and energy-producing mitochondria. The hypha then grows another cell from one end, and then another and another. But to grow into a large network, the hypha must mate by merging with another, compatible hypha.

Then hyphae form branches and extend in a web. The web keeps growing from the tips of the hyphae until it becomes a mass of white threadlike structures, known collectively as mycelium. Mycelia grow through soil, reaching, tangling, exploring, and interacting. They can spread great distances underground, like the Humongous Fungus in Oregon, transporting water and food through a network of cells and holding soil together so it does not erode. They can also grow inside a dead tree or animal, on the surface of a material, through liquid, or in living tissue.

While most fungi grow in this way, yeasts are a bit different. These single-celled fungi live together in large colonies of cells.

FUNGAL STRUCTURE

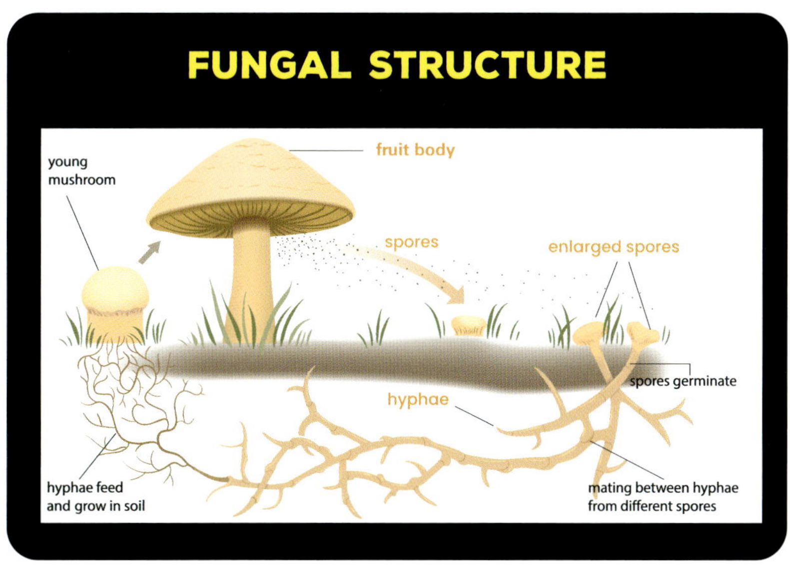

Most yeasts form a small bump on their cell surface. Internally, the cell's nucleus divides too. The bud grows bigger and bigger until it is the size of its parent cell, while the new nucleus moves inside the bud. Then a cell wall forms between the parent cell and the new cell, and the cells split apart. The yeast colony gets larger as more buds separate from their parent cells.

All fungi need to eat to grow, and they do so in a unique way. Unlike plants, fungi cannot produce their own food. They are heterotrophic organisms that need to find food in their environment, just as animals do. Yet, unlike animals, fungi don't have stomachs and digestive systems. They must digest their food outside of their bodies—and they are masterful at it. How can they do this? They grow into the food they consume. Then they exude acids and enzymes that break down the food into simple molecules that the hyphae can absorb through their cell walls. Many kinds of fungi eat dead or decaying matter, contributing to decomposition. But some feed off living organisms, and others partner with plants, feeding them and also taking nutrients from them.

SUDDENLY MUSHROOMS

As mycelia spread underground, eating and forming massive webs beneath our feet, just-right conditions make mushrooms appear seemingly overnight. This happens when the ground is wet—often after rainstorms—and hyphae fuse together. The hyphae's cells absorb water and quickly expand, bursting up through the ground and into our world as mushrooms. These mushrooms have one job to do—rapidly produce and disperse spores. And while not all fungi produce mushrooms, they have become the most well-known and studied parts of fungi, mostly because we can see them.

Many mushrooms have a cap at their top, which is at first round, cone-shaped, bell-shaped, or cup-shaped. As it matures, the cap flattens. Underneath its cap are gills, ridges, tubes, or spines. Mushrooms that have gills are agaric fungi, those with spines are tooth fungi, and the ones with tubes are bolete fungi or polypores. Supporting the cap is the mushroom's stalk. On it can be the remains of a veil, a thin tissue that covers the spore-producing parts of a new mushroom, which may protect the spores as the mushroom grows.

SPREADING SPORES

Fungi can reproduce both sexually and asexually, but mushroom-forming fungi are generally thought to only reproduce sexually. Asexual reproduction happens when a new fungus grows from fragments of hyphae, cell budding, or spores. Sexual reproduction involves hyphae from two separate fungi fusing together and creating spores. Either way, all fungi spread spores to reproduce. While molds sprout spores from the tips of their hyphae, fungi that produce fruiting bodies disperse spores in many ingenious ways. Cup-shaped mushrooms with spores lining their cups wait for water to splash inside. One of these is the bird's nest fungi, which resemble little bird's nests with egglike spore sacs inside them containing millions of spores. Splashing water hits the spore sacs, and they catapult from the bottom of the cup and stick to nearby structures, such as plant stems or leaves. Once the sac dries, it releases its spores into the air to land in a moist, shaded, woodsy place to grow.

Some mushrooms puff out clouds of spores through holes in their surface. A puffball's spores develop inside its spherical or pear-shaped body. Some giant puffballs can grow

AN ANCIENT HUMAN-FUNGAL CHRONICLE

People have been harnessing fungal power since our earliest days. From food to fire starters and mystical to medicinal, here are some ways ancient peoples used fungi throughout the millennia.

17,000 BCE: THE RED LADY

El Mirón Cave in Cantabria, Spain, holds the earliest proof of human fungal use yet—and the proof was discovered in dental plaque! The Red Lady is an adult woman who was formally buried inside the cave about nineteen thousand years ago. Her people were hunter-gatherers who foraged the land and hunted animals for food. Scientists studied samples from the dark coating on her teeth and found intact and identifiable fungal spores. They included spores from bolete (also known as porcini) and agaric mushrooms.

3300 BCE: ÖTZI, THE ICEMAN

Found frozen and mummified in the mountains of northern Italy, Ötzi the Iceman is an astonishingly well-preserved person from the Copper Age (3500–2300 BCE)—older than the Egyptian pyramids and Stonehenge. Some of his clothing and equipment were

to 2 feet (0.6 m) in diameter and hold seven trillion spores. To spread, the surface of giant puffballs disintegrates and exposes their spores to the environment where they are blown away by wind and rain. Other mushrooms need an outside force to release their spores. Raindrops or small animals can provide that force, pushing down on the mushroom's surface and releasing a cloud of spores into the air, just like a puff of smoke.

Spore shooters are fungi that explosively eject spores like cannonballs. Hat-thrower fungi (*Pilobolus*) grow on animal dung and need to pass through animals' bodies as part of their life cycle. Yet most animals don't eat near dung. So, these fungi preserved too, and among these items were a few kinds of fungi. Inside a pouch on his belt was a piece of tinder fungus, which grows on birch trees and can smolder for days, holding a spark to start a fire. The Iceman also had birch fungus tied to leather strips, which can be used as medicine to relieve pain or fight infection.

300 BCE: MUSHROOM CULTS

Found at ancient Maya sites in Guatemala are peculiar stone carvings. Many look like people with mushroom-shaped caps on their heads. These mushroom stones are thought to have been religious statues. Ancient Maya and Aztecs consumed mushrooms that produced hallucinations, which were believed to be visions from their gods.

25–220 CE: A MEDICAL COMPENDIUM

The book *Shen Nong Ben Cao Jing* was written during the Han dynasty (206 BCE–220 CE) of ancient China. It is the first book to describe the medicinal value of different herbs and plants. It includes the medicinal uses of several kinds of mushrooms, including Ling Zhi (also called reishi). This mushroom has long been revered in China, Japan, and other Asian countries for promoting longevity and good physical health.

evolved mechanisms that shoot their spores away from their dung homes. Instead of mushrooms, they grow special hyphae into the air called sporangiophores. Inside sacs at the end of the sporangiophores are clusters of spores. Sunlight heats liquid inside, and as it expands, the liquid creates pressure that pushes on the sporangiophores until they explode and shoot sticky spore clusters into the air, some traveling at speeds of up to 56 miles (90 km) per hour and landing 10 feet (3 m) away! They stick to plants, which animals eat, and then travel through the animals' bodies and come out in their dung—the fungus's ideal home. The artillery fungus (*Sphaerobolus stellatus*), meanwhile, fires its spores from a fruiting body that splits open, revealing a mass of spores above a membrane. Five hours later, the membrane rapidly moves up to fire out a black cannonball of spores, traveling up to 20 feet (6 m) away and sticking to whatever is in its path.

Flies and beetles can't resist the smell of rotting animals or feces. Stinkhorn mushrooms use this to their advantage. These mushrooms look odd, like pointed towers, octopus arms, or latticed balls. They release a cocktail of chemicals that smell rotten and deathlike (hence their name), attracting the insects that eat their spore mass. Then, when the insects later release their waste, the spores travel with it and into a new hospitable place to grow.

Many mushrooms use gravity's help to spread their spores. These mushrooms have gills, ridges, pores, or teethlike growths that point toward the ground from their caps. Inside, dusty spores shoot out at high speeds and then rain down, catching the wind or riding on water until they find a new home. Each mushroom can release up to one billion spores each day! Studies even show that fungi give their spores an aerial boost by cooling the air around them. Fungi are usually cool to the touch. How do they keep their cool temperatures? They rapidly release water into the air through evaporation, cooling the air around them by several degrees. This cooler air is denser than the warmer air around it, meaning it has more molecules putting pressure on objects in the air. This pressure pushes up on the spores and helps them travel farther in the warmer and less dense air around the mushroom.

FUNKY AND FANTASTIC

Mushrooms form in a dazzling array of shapes, sizes, and colors. Some are bloodred, some glow an eerie green, and

Molds produce lightweight spores on the tip of their hyphae and release them. Wind, animals, and people can then carry the mold to new locations.

many are shades of earthy browns, beiges, and oranges. They have spotted or scaly caps and can be fuzzy or smooth. They grow out of the sides of trees like shelves or hang, dripping, like a fuzzy white beard. They can be coated in slime, oozing and sticky . . . dry and woody . . . branched like coral . . . or spongy and velvety soft. Some even seep a red sap that looks like little drops of blood!

All kinds of fungi and their mushrooms are out there—some discovered but many yet to be found. Their forms, colors, and behaviors vary widely, and scientists make many new and unusual discoveries every year. Some mushrooms are delicate, fragile, and exquisitely ornate. Many are delicious treasures, valued by foodies and chefs for their aroma and taste. Others can kill in the most horrifying ways or change minds and help people heal.

Surveying the species provides a sense of the diversity of fungi and the many ways they have evolved within our world.

CHAPTER 2

THE BEAUTIES

While our compendium of fungi keeps growing as new discoveries are made, what we do know already is that fungi come in many unique forms. Some of their mushrooms, such as the mauve parachute or hairy trumpet, are delicately beautiful, spindly, and whimsical, with candy-like colors as if they're from fairy tales. Others look as if they come straight out of a horror film—seemingly bloody and emanating death and foulness, with equally horrific names such as the bleeding tooth or devil's fingers. First let's look at some of the rare and dazzling beauties of the fungal world.

MAUVE PARACHUTE OR PURPLE PINWHEEL

Scientific name:
Marasmius haematocephalus

GEOGRAPHIC LOCATIONS: US, Central and South America, Asia, New Zealand, Papua New Guinea, Java, Malaysia, Sri Lanka, Thailand, Cameroon, Democratic Republic of Congo, Gabon, Ghana, Ivory Coast, Kenya, Nigeria, Republic of the Congo, Sierra Leone, Tanzania, Uganda, Zimbabwe

HABITAT: leaf litter and dead twigs on the floor of subtropical and tropical forests

GILLS: up to fourteen spaced gills that are white with pink borders

SPORES: white

This small, delicate agaric mushroom has a spindly dark pink-and-black stem that grows up to about 2 inches (60 mm) tall and 0.03 inches (1 mm) in diameter (think wiry and hairlike). Its dark pink, bell-shaped cap is slightly velvety and up to 0.4 inches (10 mm) in diameter, or about the size of a dime. Its flesh is thin and tough, and it's inedible. The mauve parachute is known for its reviving ability—it shrivels up when it's dry out and then springs back to life when it rains. *Marasmius* originates from the Greek word *marasmos*, meaning "drying out."

SPLIT-GILL MUSHROOM

Scientific name:
Schizophyllum commune

GEOGRAPHIC LOCATION: all over the world except Antarctica

HABITAT: forests with hardwood logs and branches, mostly dead trees but some living

FOLDS: gill-like folds with a split down the center

SPORES: white

This beautiful, small, fan-shaped white bracket fungus is one of the most common kinds of fungi. It has a densely hairy cap and no stalk, growing like a tiny shelf from the sides of hardwood trees. It contains compounds that activate the immune system, and people in parts of Asia have used it for centuries to make an immunity-boosting tonic. And incredibly, scientists have discovered that this fungus has up to twenty-eight thousand distinct sexes! Its mycelium only produce one fruiting body per year. The mushroom can go dormant during dry spells, closing its folds to protect spore-making bodies inside—a unique ability in the fungal world. Then it can reactivate when conditions are moist, opening its folds again. Although rare, it has also infected immunocompromised people, forming fruiting bodies or masses inside their sinuses or lungs.

HAIRY TRUMPET

Scientific name:
Panus fasciatus

GEOGRAPHIC LOCATION: Australia, Central Africa, Brazil

HABITAT: dead trees in forests

GILLS: underneath its cap

SPORES: white

This unusual mushroom has a distinct funnel-shaped cap when it's young, which then flattens as it matures. It starts out a purply color and turns brown, and it has a velvety surface covered with delicate hairs.

FUNGAL ADVENTURER AND SCIENTIST: DR. JESSIE UEHLING

While Dr. Jessie Uehling runs a mycology laboratory and bases her fungal research out of Oregon State University, her studies have taken her around the world. She searches for new kinds of fungi to better understand how they interact with organisms and how those interactions drive evolution and fungal diversity. She's been to the countries of Guyana and Cameroon and US states including Idaho, California, and North Carolina to study fungi. "My studies started documenting the mushroom diversity in the rainforests of South America and Africa," she explained, "and then shifted into some of the pioneering work on describing the fungal microbiome. More recently I have been working to understand Pacific Northwest fungal diversity, studying the medicinal effects and biology of *Ganoderma* species (sometimes called reishi or Ling Zhi)." She's also been studying mushrooms containing the psychedelic compound psilocybin for therapeutic uses to treat mental health issues.

Uehling's research team has discovered several fungal species too. They include several *Clavulina* species, found in the tropical

Uehling examines a mushroom on the forest floor.

rainforests of the Guiana Shield region in South America. A few others are *Cantharellus guyanensis* and *Craterellus cinereofimbriatus*. Uehling has also done some exciting fieldwork in Guyana and French Guiana. "We had a basecamp at the base of Mt. Ayanganna and were studying fungi that are symbiotic with special ancient trees in the genus *Dicymbe* that grow in that region," she explained. "I was collecting and sequencing DNA from plant-associated fungi and root tips under those trees to understand which fungi are there and if those species are new to science. There are so many amazing and beautiful fungi in the tropics!"

Since she was young, Uehling has always wanted to be a mycologist. Her upbringing helped. She said, "I grew up in Idaho, so playing in the forest and camping and hiking had a big impact on my career choice. My mother was a professor and my father was a highly skilled outdoors person, so in hindsight my career is a blend of what they exposed me to." To achieve her career aspirations, Uehling geared her education toward the sciences, taking "AP science courses like chemistry and biology that prepared me for college level science classes." In graduate school at Duke University (a mycological research hub) in North Carolina, she met "one of my most influential mentors, Professor Rytas Vilgalys, who taught me to unapologetically follow my passion for fungi and give back as generously as possible to the mycological community, which I call the mycofam."

For future mycologists thinking about how to get into the field, Uehling advises to "try to get research experience by doing an internship or working in a lab as soon as possible. If there are any scientific research conferences in your region, see if you can get a scholarship from the hosting society to attend part or all and find people doing research you're interested [in] to ask questions to. Meeting in person to discuss science is a big part of career development."

VIOLET CORAL

Scientific name:
Clavaria zollingeri

GEOGRAPHIC LOCATION: North America, Europe, South America, Asia, Australia, New Zealand

HABITAT: grasslands and woodlands—in moss under hardwood trees and on the ground

BRANCHES: spores release from the tips of each prong

SPORES: white

Like tiny purple antlers, this mushroom grows from the ground as a central body and branches into many prongs. If it were in the ocean, you might mistake it for coral. It is one of many kinds of coral fungi, which are usually bright and inedible. This beautiful specimen grows up to 4 inches (10 cm) tall and 3 inches (7.6 cm) wide, alone or in groupings. It starts out violet and then browns as it ages. Instead of a cap and gills, it has prongs tipped with spore-producing cells (basidia), which each shoot four spores into the air.

PARROT WAXCAP OR PARROT TOADSTOOL

Scientific name:
Gliophorus psittacinus

GEOGRAPHIC LOCATION: Europe, North America

HABITAT: mossy areas, grasslands, hardwood or conifer forests

GILLS: thick, widely spaced gills that are mostly yellow and pale green

SPORES: white

Covered in slime, this tiny, umbrellalike mushroom gets its name from the Greek words *glia* (meaning "glue") and *phoros* (meaning "bearing"). Just like a parrot's feathers, its cap is emerald green. It tops a bright yellow stalk, and as the mushroom matures, its cap turns yellow too. It reaches just over 2 inches (5 cm) high, and its cap is about 1.7 inches (4.3 cm) wide. It's believed to be inedible (but, if not, is at least undesirable to eat) and is hard to pick too, due to its extreme sliminess.

CAESAR'S MUSHROOM

Scientific names:
Amanita caesarea, Amanita hemibapha,* and *Amanita jacksonii

GEOGRAPHIC LOCATION: North America, Central America, Europe, Northern Africa

HABITAT: pine and oak forests

GILLS: pale yellow, thinly spaced, not attached to the stem

SPORES: white

Some *Amanita* mushrooms are deadly—so toxic that they can make a person's organs shut down. But, surprisingly, the *Amanita caesarea* is edible, and many people think it's delicious. It was even one of Roman emperor Julius Caesar's favorite mushrooms to eat! It grows from an egglike veil sac called the volva that breaks open as the mushroom's cap expands. It has a stunning red, orange, and yellow cap that begins as an oval egg and flattens as it matures. Striations line the cap's edges, and the remnant of its veil remains on its up to 6-inch (15 cm) stalk.

INDIGO MILK CAP

Scientific name:
Lactarius indigo

GEOGRAPHIC LOCATION: North America, Central America

HABITAT: oak and pine forests

GILLS: blue, thinly spaced gills that attach to the stem

SPORES: cream

Blue fungi are rare, but the indigo milk cap is one of them. This unusually beautiful and vibrant mushroom is hard to miss in the forest. It is the fruiting body of symbiotic fungi that support their host oak and pine trees by supplying nutrients and water and receiving carbohydrates (sugars) in exchange. If you cut or scrape the mushroom's flesh, a milky, blue liquid called latex oozes out and turns dark green as it interacts with oxygen in the air. The mushroom has a hollow body and a large, concave cap.

CHAPTER 3

THE ODDITIES

Some mushrooms look like alien life—so odd and unusual that it can seem as if you've stepped onto another planet when you suddenly find yourself among a grouping of them in a forest. Just imagine being surrounded by giant white balls among the trees. They puff out clouds of spores and seem to pop out of nowhere on the forest floor. Or what if suddenly bloodred tentacles reaching into the air surrounded you, emitting a stench so awful it makes you sick? These mushrooms belong to the oddities of the fungi family, and there are many members. Take a look, maybe a few—you might be surprised at these strange fungal specimens.

RED CAGE FUNGUS, BASKET STINKHORN

Scientific name:
Clathrus ruber

GEOGRAPHIC LOCATION: Asia, North America, Central America, Australia, Europe, Mediterranean

HABITAT: near woody debris; in gardens, lawns, farms

GLEBA: a sticky slime that holds spores

SPORES: brown

Bursting from an off-white, egglike sac covered in a geometric pattern, the red cage fungus expands into a hollow, latticed ball stained red, orange, or pink. Its coloring comes from carotene, the same pigment that makes a carrot orange. Inside its latticed frame is its gleba, a sticky, dark green slime containing the spores. Here is where its putrid stench comes from. It smells like a dead animal on a hot, sunny day. This attracts flies and other insects, who eat and transport the gleba. Wherever the flies go, the red cage's spores drop off their bodies to find new homes below. About twenty-four hours after it emerges, the fungus's latticed ball collapses and sinks back into the ground it came from.

LION'S MANE, MONKEY HEAD MUSHROOM

Scientific name:
Hericium erinaceus

GEOGRAPHIC LOCATION: North America, Asia, Europe

HABITAT: dying or dead hardwood trees

TEETH/SPINES: growing down from its body and hanging like a lion's mane or hair

SPORES: white, shot from tissue around each tooth/spine

No other fungus looks quite like the lion's mane, with its shaggy, beardlike fruiting bodies. It has long been prized as a delicious, edible fungus that some people also believe has medicinal qualities. It's been used in Chinese medicine for centuries and may help with digestion, internal organ health, vitality, and strength. Some studies have shown that lion's mane has great potential in medicine for its anticancer and brain health benefits, and researchers are looking into using it for Alzheimer's disease, Parkinson's disease, and cancer treatments. When eaten, it is a good meat substitute. Some say it tastes and chews like crab.

FLOR DE COCO (COCONUT FLOWER)

Scientific name:
Neonothopanus gardneri

GEOGRAPHIC LOCATION: Brazil

HABITAT: decaying palm trees

GILLS: pale yellow and widely spaced gills under the cap and onto the stalk

SPORES: white

On dark nights in parts of Brazil, neon-green organisms glow at the base of palm trees. Local residents named them coconut flowers, but they are not flowers. They are bioluminescent mushrooms. The species is one of about one hundred known bioluminescent mushrooms, and it is the brightest of them all. It makes its chemical light by combining three ingredients: the light-emitting compound luciferin and the enzymes reductase and luciferase. Why does it glow? Scientists tested the fungus and found that it regulated its light by monitoring the temperature. Its lights only come on at night, when rove beetles, flies, and other insects attracted to light sources are active. Some think the fungus uses light to attract spore-spreading insects. Since it grows under the forest's tree canopy with little wind, insects may be the best way for the fungus to disperse its spores.

ILLUMINATING THE *TURTLE*

During the Revolutionary War (1775–1783), the American colonies were looking for ingenious ways to outsmart their enemy. A young Yale University student, David Bushnell, came up with something completely new—the world's first combat submarine, the *Turtle*. He thought the colonies could use it to break the British blockade of Boston Harbor by delivering underwater explosives to British ships. The vessel was made from two wooden-domed ovals (kind of like turtle shells) fastened together with iron hoops and waterproofed with pine-tar pitch (a sticky material made from pine sap). It had just enough room for one person to operate it using pedals and gears.

But there was a problem—Bushnell needed a way to illuminate the control panel. It was dark underwater, electric light was not yet an option for a vehicle such as this, and the flame of a candle would consume valuable oxygen an operator needed to breathe. Yet, without light, an operator would not be able to steer the submarine toward the enemy.

What was Bushnell's solution? Bioluminescent fungi, or foxfire as it was called then, which grew in wood. Benjamin Gale, Bushnell's colleague at Yale, tells how it was used: "On the inside is fixed a Barometer, by which [the operator] can tell the depth he is under water; a Compass, by which he knows the course he steers. In the barometer and on the needles of the compass is fixed *fox-fire*, i.e. wood that gives light in the dark." And although the *Turtle* never succeeded in battle, it did show how fungi could be an inventive solution for a seemingly impossible problem.

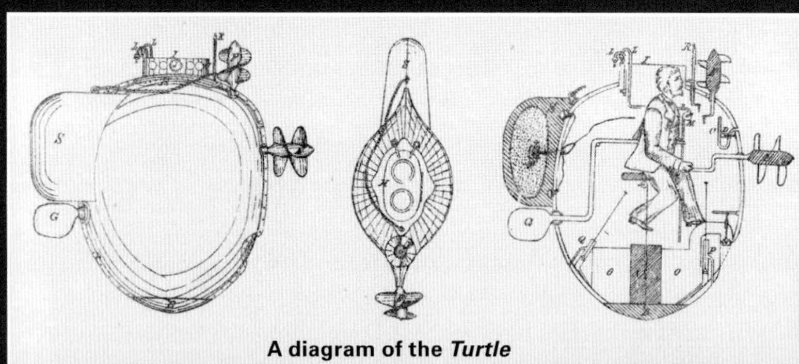

A diagram of the *Turtle*

DEVIL'S FINGERS, OCTOPUS STINKHORN

Scientific name:
Clathrus archeri

GEOGRAPHIC LOCATION: Australia, New Zealand, North America, Europe, Asia

HABITAT: tree stumps, woodland floors, damp grassland

GLEBA: a sticky slime that holds spores

SPORES: olive brown or green

Probably the most alien-like of them all, devil's fingers reach out of the ground with their red and black branches, which look a bit like a blood-soaked octopus's tentacles. This fungus is another member of the stinkhorn family that grows inside a white, gelatinous, egglike sac. When its spores are developed, the arms burst out of the egg still clumped together. They rise and then split apart, curving back down toward the ground. Dark gleba filled with spores coats each arm, and the mushroom emits a foul stench that smells like rotting dead animals and feces. That smell is like honey to flies and other insects, which eat the sticky gleba. Spores stick to their wings and bodies. Then the spores fall off as the insects visit other areas. That's how this creepy fungus spreads.

THE STINK OF STINKHORNS

How do stinkhorns earn their name? They use a stinky chemical cocktail, of course. In 2014 a group of researchers in Prague studied stinkhorns' smell and identified the volatile compounds they emit. Dimethyl oligosulphides were the main chemical culprits. These chemicals were only present when the fruiting body was mature, not when it was young. They create an aroma reminiscent of rotting flesh, feces, and cabbage. Within this group, the stinkiest is dimethyl trisulfide. Fun fact: It is also one of the chemicals that makes the giant corpse flower smell like dead bodies!

The bridal veil stinkhorn is named for its webbed white veil.

BLEEDING TOOTH FUNGUS, DEVIL'S TOOTH, STRAWBERRIES AND CREAM

Scientific name:
Hydnellum peckii

GEOGRAPHIC LOCATION: North America, Europe, Australia, Korea, Iran

HABITAT: coniferous forest floors, often on pine trees

TEETH/SPINES: grow down from its body

SPORES: brown

A young bleeding tooth fungus is hard to miss on the forest floor. Its bright white, lumpy body seeps bloodred droplets of liquid on its surface. But this liquid is not a kind of blood but more like a sap. Called guttation, the sweating of this sap happens when the fungus sits on a soaked surface and absorbs too much water. The liquid creates pressure inside the fungus's fruiting body and pushes up until it's forced out. A pigment inside the fungus turns the liquid red. Even though they aren't actually bloody, extracts from the fungus can help human blood. The fungus contains an anticoagulant called atromentin, which can prevent blood clots from forming and, with its antibacterial aspects, help treat bacterial pneumonia.

ZOMBIE-ANT FUNGUS

Scientific name:
Ophiocordyceps unilateralis

GEOGRAPHIC LOCATION: Brazil, Thailand

HABITAT: tropical rainforest trees

PORES: spores are squeezed out through pores of a bulbous fruiting body

SPORES: white

Imagine a fungus that can take over your body, make you go places you don't usually go, and then send a fruiting body straight through your head. No, it's not the plot of a gross zombie horror movie—it's what the zombie-ant fungus does to ants! In tropical rainforests, a spore lands on a foraging carpenter ant walking on the forest floor. It excretes enzymes that break through the ant's exoskeleton and begins growing inside the ant's body. Its hyphae wrap around the ant's muscles. Soon the ant starts acting strangely. It leaves its nest in the tree canopy, it walks without direction, and it twitches until it falls to the ground. Then it finds a plant with a leaf that's about

FUNGI ON FUNGI

Not all fungi grow on trees or in the ground. Some fungi are parasites of other fungi—they live off other fungal species! Mycoparasitism is fairly common in the fungal world. Some fungal parasites kill their hosts, while others coexist with living hosts. One is *Hypomyces lactifluorum*, or the lobster mushroom. It grows over the surface and into the tissue of existing *Russula* fungi, turning their mushrooms a bright orange red (just like the shell of cooked lobster). The lobster mushroom drastically changes its host—the host's tissue becomes mummified, its shape and smell change, and its gills turn into blunt ridges. This makes the host mushroom delicious. A Canadian study showed that the lobster mushroom turns the unpalatable host *Russula brevipes* into a delicious mushroom by mostly replacing its host's DNA and changing its metabolites (which determine how fungi look, taste, and whether they are edible).

10 inches (25 cm) off the ground and facing north. That spot has just the right humidity and temperature for the fungus to grow. The ant climbs up to the underside of the leaf and locks its jaws in a death grip on the leaf's main vein.

Then the fungus completely takes over. Its hyphae wind through and grow out of the ant's body, gluing it to the leaf as the fungus digests and kills the ant. Within a week, a stalk grows out of the back of the ant's head, and a fruiting body forms, facing the ground. Then spores rain down to unsuspecting ants below so the whole cycle can start again. Scientists think the fungus controls the ant's muscles using its mycelial network sort of like how a puppeteer uses strings and then excretes chemicals to control the ant's movements. The effectiveness of this control is surprising, as the ant ends up in just the right spot for the fungus to thrive without using the thinking power of the ant's brain.

It was December 2007, and Cristiano Savini and his father, Luciano, were looking for something underground in a forest near the roots of the trees that grew there. Their dog, Rocco, was smelling the ground for what he had been trained to detect. Suddenly, the dog started sniffing excitedly, focused on one area. Cristiano and his father tied Rocco to a nearby tree so the dog wouldn't dig and destroy his precious discovery. Then the two men carefully dug into the ground to unearth a lumpy white mass that weighed approximately 3.3 pounds (1.5 kg). It was the aromatic fruiting body of a fungus and one of the most prized ingredients for foodies around the world—a white truffle.

The Savinis are known for finding truffles, and their family business has been selling them for more than one hundred

The Savini family are experienced truffle hunters. In 2007 Cristiano unearthed another large truffle just one month before their famous December find.

years. Yet this truffle was truly special. It was one of the largest ever found. They knew it would attract attention and sell for an enormous price. Truffles are expensive, and most sell for $5,500 per 1 pound (0.5 kg), although they usually only weigh in around 1 to 3 ounces (28 to 85 g). Chefs use this expensive ingredient sparingly, with just thinly shaved slivers to flavor their dishes.

The family took their truffle to auction and decided to donate the proceeds to charity. When it went on the auction block (simultaneously broadcast in Florence, Italy; London, England; and Macau, China), no one could have expected the price it would fetch. Billionaire casino mogul Stanley Ho was the winning bidder, paying a staggering $330,000 for the truffle, making it one of the most expensive truffles ever sold in the world. And white truffles, prized as they are for their flavor and aroma, stay fresh for less than *one week*.

MEATY, BUBBLY, AND MOLDY

Truffles are the most expensive kinds of fungi (and maybe the hardest to find, unless you have a good nose), although many mushrooms have long been valued for their flavor and nutritional value. They are rich in protein, fiber, vitamins, and antioxidants, while also being low in fat and calories. They also have a rich, savory flavor that chefs often use to add umami, the fifth taste (the other four being salty, sweet, sour, and bitter). Due to their umami flavor and meatlike texture, many people use mushrooms as a meat substitute, with portobello, chicken of the woods, and oyster mushrooms as some favorite picks. Only a small number of mushroom species are commonly grown and eaten, though, including the common button, enoki, shiitake, morel, and oyster. Many animals eat mushrooms as part of their diets too—pigs, bears, squirrels, and deer, to name a few.

Ancient peoples foraged for mushrooms as part of their diets (like the Red Lady in Spain), and modern people have been using other fungi in food and drinks for many thousands of years too. If you asked someone more than a few hundred years ago what made their juice turn into wine, dough rise to make fluffy bread, soybeans and wheat become soy sauce, or cheese develop pungent flavor, you might have gotten a blank stare. People used yeasts and molds in their foods without even knowing it—it was likely an accidental discovery. Yet these fungi were essential to making the many basic food and drink products that comprised their diets.

People have been fermenting foods for thousands of years. Beer, a lightly alcoholic and carbonated drink made through fermentation, is one. Microorganisms such as yeast carry out the chemical process of fermentation. The microorganism consumes sugars in the mashed-up grains used for beer. Then it releases water, alcohol, and carbon dioxide (which makes the drink bubbly), and the mixture becomes beer. Yeast changes grape juice to wine like this too. A similar process happens when making bread dough. When the dough is left to rise, the yeast produces big air pockets inside the dough after consuming sugar. These air pockets make the bread light and airy when the dough is baked.

BUBBLING BEER

Remnants of beer-making tools used by the Natufian people and traces of the drink from about thirteen thousand years ago were discovered in Raqefet Cave in modern Israel. Traces of beer in pottery vessels from nine thousand years ago were discovered in China, along with the mold and yeast that fermented its ingredients. Ancient Sumerians and Babylonians in Mesopotamia documented making beer on clay tablets over six thousand to seven thousand years ago. Archaeologists have also found beer residue inside their clay vessels. In ancient Egypt, beer was an essential part of the diet. Hieroglyphics and wooden sculptures found in tombs show people brewing and drinking the beverage. And although their beer was likely nothing like modern-day beer, fermentation was still a necessary part of the process.

FERMENTING SOYBEANS

Soybeans are used to make fermented foods that have been in production in East Asia for thousands of years. They were made into a paste called jiang, which was first documented in the ancient Chinese text *Analects of Confucious* that's estimated

FIGURING OUT FERMENTATION

While people had been using fermentation for thousands of years, for a long time, no one knew what really made it happen. That is until French chemist Louis Pasteur figured it out in the mid-1800s. At that time, many people believed in the idea of spontaneous generation (that certain living organisms could come alive from nonliving matter, such as maggots appearing in the flesh of dead animals). It was thought to explain certain mysterious processes, such as fermentation. But Pasteur and some of his colleagues believed that tiny organisms that no one could see were responsible. So, Pasteur performed controlled experiments using microscopes to understand the role of yeast in alcohol production. He saw that yeast multiplication and fermentation both increased at the same time. He concluded that fermentation was a result of yeast multiplication—and yeast needed to be alive to multiply. He published an early paper about it in 1857 and another confirming his findings in 1860.

to have been completed about 200 BCE. Early varieties of jiang had been made with seafood and other ingredients. But as jiang evolved in China, its main ingredients became soybeans, a salt solution, and a mixture of molds that grew on soaked wheat grains and were used to make wine. After it was left to ferment for at least one hundred days, it became a thick liquid that the ancient Chinese people used to preserve other foods, such as tofu, melon, and pork. Another product later made from jiang was a salty liquid produced during its fermentation—jiang-you, or soy sauce. It started the same way as jiang and was mixed with salt water in large clay pots. The pots were set outside in the sunshine, which sped up the fermentation process, and

Other regions, such as Japan, also ferment soy sauce in large barrels. Some artisan makers let it ferment for between one and three years.

mixed daily for between three and six months. The dark liquid produced was then strained and further aged in smaller pots. This complicated process was made possible through the cultivation of two kinds of molds—*Aspergillus* and *Rhizopus*. This tasty sauce became an essential Chinese seasoning, later spread to Japan and Korea, and has since spread around the world, with each country adding variations to the process. Fermented soybeans are now essential to many other foods too, such as miso and pickled tofu.

RISEN BREAD

The yeast *Saccharomyces cerevisiae* is responsible for the fluffy leavened bread that many people enjoy. Yeast is just a single cell, but it works hard when given the right conditions. It consumes sugars found in grains and fruit and uses oxygen to produce ethanol (or alcohol) and carbon dioxide. When mixed into bread dough and left out in a warm environment, yeast makes dough grow. Gluten, which forms when wheat's protein mixes with water, acts as a stretchy net in the dough. It traps the carbon dioxide bubbles inside the dough, while also allowing it to expand. As the carbon dioxide pushes up, the dough rises. Together, yeast and gluten result in a dough filled with airy gaps that then bakes into a light and fluffy loaf of bread.

The earliest evidence of leavened bread comes from ancient Egypt, where bread was a basic dietary staple. Archaeologists have found sculptures and painted scenes in tombs depicting bakeries. They have also found extremely stale but intact loaves of bread preserved in the arid desert conditions of Egypt, often in tombs as offerings to the dead. In 1996 results from a study on seventy of these loaves were published. Archaeologists had found bread loaves at the workers' villages of Deir el-Medina (dated at 1550 to 1307 BCE) and Amarna (dated about 1350 BCE). Researchers studied the loaves using scanning electron microscopy, a microscope that focuses a stream of electrons on an object to make a magnified, detailed image of its surface. The results showed yeast cells on the surface of bread loaves baked with emmer grain, the first evidence of yeast's use in bread.

MOLDY CHEESE

While moldy cheese might not sound so tasty, if it's the right kind of mold, it might be just what a cheesemaker wants. Blue cheeses need mold to achieve their distinctively funky taste, look, and smell, but it needs to be the mold *Penicillium roqueforti*. While many molds are harmful to people, this mold does not make toxins. The cheeses that rely on this fungus include Roquefort, Gorgonzola, and Stilton, among others. The mold grows through the cheese to create a web of blue veins. It releases enzymes that then release amino acids, which break down proteins in the cheese to make it creamy and soft. Another by-product of the fungus is methyl ketone, which gives the cheese a sharp taste, blue color, and pungent smell.

While some myths tell that blue cheese resulted after a young man abandoned his bread and cheese in a cave in France, only to return months later to find blue cheese, no one knows for sure how this kind of cheese originated. But a discovery in the Austrian Alps has provided an unexpected clue to the early production of blue cheese. Inside the world's oldest salt mines at Hallstatt were some very well-preserved paleofeces (or ancient human poop) left by miners working there, some samples dating back to 1301 BCE. In 2021 scientists used microscopic and molecular analysis to examine the paleofeces and better understand the miners' diets, and they found something interesting from a sample dating to between 650–545 BCE, an early period of the Iron Age (1200 BCE–1000 CE). It included high concentrations of *Penicillium roqueforti*, suggesting that the miners ate blue cheese close to three thousand years ago. That meant Iron Age people were producing blue cheese long before anyone thought the cheese was being made. The discovery surprised the study's lead scientist, Frank Maixner, who said, "This is very sophisticated in my opinion . . . something I did not expect at that time. The Hallstatt miners seem to have intentionally applied food fermentation technologies with microorganisms which are still nowadays used in the food industry."

MUSHROOMS: UMAMI MAKERS

One of the more obvious ways we eat fungi is by using mushrooms as an ingredient in our food. People have foraged for wild mushrooms for thousands of years, but farming mushrooms is a relatively newer practice. The most basic one likely almost everyone has encountered in their local grocery store is the white button mushroom, *Agaricus bisporus*. It was first grown in France in 1600 and then began to be commercially produced there in 1780. In the United States, the first commercial production of white button mushrooms started in Pennsylvania in 1894, inside a building specially designed to grow mushrooms. Now these mushrooms are the most

FARMING FUNGI

A fungi farm is not your typical farm—you won't see rows of mushrooms sprouting in a field. Instead, commercial mushroom cultivation usually occurs in a controlled environment, such as a building where humidity, temperature, and nutrients can be monitored and adjusted. Growing indoors also allows farmers to produce mushrooms year-round, while outdoor farms only produce seasonal crops. At a fungi farm, it's all about feeding the mycelium with the right substrate and providing the right environment to promote the production of fruiting bodies. Most farmers grow mushrooms in trays, but they can also use bags, buckets, logs, and jars. Substrates are made from natural products, including straw, sawdust, manure, cocoa bean hulls, coffee grounds, and gypsum. Farmers inoculate (inject) the substrate with spawn, spores that have grown mycelium over grain. This produces a consistent crop of mushrooms.

common kind found in US and European stores, prized for their mild taste whether eaten raw or cooked.

Since commercial production began in the 1700s, more and more kinds of mushrooms are being commercially produced and sold at stores. Some of the more popular ones are the large-capped portobello mushrooms, which have a darker color and meaty texture, and cremini mushrooms, which are just baby portobellos. Often food co-ops or natural food stores sell some of the less common types—morels, chanterelle, porcini, and more. Some stores also sell lion's mane or chicken of the woods mushrooms. For vegetarians and vegans, mushrooms can be a delicious source of protein and nutrients and provide good texture in recipes, and some companies now make alternative meat products from fungi.

While relatively new in US stores, many other kinds of mushrooms have long been used in Asian cuisine to add umami to recipes. They include shiitake, oyster, and enoki mushrooms, among others, some of which have been cultivated for hundreds of years. Shiitake mushrooms are the second most cultivated mushroom in the world and were first grown in China about one thousand years ago. A woodcutter named Wu San Kwung is credited for first cultivating this mushroom, which grows on logs. The mushrooms were later introduced to Japan, which has become the world leader in shiitake cultivation.

TRUFFLES: UNDERGROUND TREASURES

Some of the hardest to find fruiting bodies are truffles, simply because we cannot see them. The kinds used in gourmet dishes, such as black and white truffles, need to be smelled to be found. They grow underground by tree roots—usually oak, beech, birch,

HOW TO TRAIN A TRUFFLE HOUND

Truffle hunting does not come naturally to dogs (as it does for pigs), so they need to be trained. Here's how dogs become the best truffle hunters.

1. Get your dog used to the smell of truffles while also receiving a treat. Your dog will then associate truffles with rewards.
2. Start getting your dog used to finding truffles outside. Take your dog to an enclosed outdoor area. Let them explore.
3. Bury some truffles in shallow holes for your dog to find. Give your dog a treat when they find the truffle.
4. Bring your dog out every day before dinner to find more truffles in the enclosed area. Bury the truffles a little deeper to make them harder to find. Always give treats after your dog finds a truffle.
5. Keep working and your dog will get better and better at finding truffles. Just make sure they do not eat them! Then take your dog out into a forest where truffles are found to put their training to the test.

poplar, and pine trees—and form a symbiotic relationship with them. While the trees provide sugar that they photosynthesize from the sunlight, the truffles provide extra water and nutrients to the trees. The truffles have no stalks and form a lumpy round mass that grows only during certain seasons.

Since these fungal fruiting bodies grow underground, they cannot use the wind or water to distribute their spores. Instead, they emit a strong scent—one that certain animals find irresistible, leading them to eat the mushroom and then spread the spores as they leave droppings wherever they go. Truffle hunters have specially trained animals to help them find the fungi. Dogs and pigs have the best noses for truffles. Pigs were

Desert truffles are another popular variety. They may look different from white and black truffles, but people still use them in many tasty dishes.

the first used because they have such a good sense of smell and naturally love to eat the fungi. That was the problem with pigs, though. They often ate the truffles themselves and badly damaged the ground where they grew. So, trained dogs (that don't naturally want to eat truffles) are the more popular choice now, and the Lagotti Romagnoli breed is especially good at it.

Italy, France, and the US Pacific Northwest are known for their truffle-producing forests. The hunters go to forests that they know have the trees known to support the fungi. The best times to look are after heavy rainfall in winter or summer. The dogs lead, sniffing the ground for the truffle's scent, and then alert their owners when they smell something. Then the humans take over and use a special spade that does not harm the soil around the truffle's hiding spot to dig it out. The fresh truffles then need to be eaten within a week (or less), as they spoil quickly. Black truffles are easier to find and prized for their earthy taste. They are eaten either shaved raw or cooked and can also be farmed. White truffles are rare and have a pungent flavor. They are eaten

LIGHTNING AND TRUFFLES

Desert truffle hunters often say that lightning storms bring out the best crops of truffles. Yet no one has proved this to be true. Some think the lightning triggers a chemical reaction in the rainwater. This might make the water rich in nitrogen, an important nutrient for mushrooms. Truffle hunters believe if there is no lightning, they will not find many desert truffles that season.

raw and are extremely difficult to farm due to their symbiotic relationships with trees.

Desert truffles are very different from their gourmet cousins. They can be quite big, look a bit like lumpy potatoes, and are fairly easy to find. They have a milder flavor and are always eaten cooked, often roasted in a fire's coals. Nomadic peoples have eaten truffles as an important protein source for at least four thousand years. They are nutritious—containing about 27 percent protein, 28 percent carbohydrates, 7 percent fat, and fiber and amino acids. They grow in the desert by the raqrooq plant (also called the sunrose or rock rose) and are common in Saudi Arabia, Iraq, Syria, Algeria, Libya, and Mauritania. People look for them after heavy rainfalls and thunderstorms, searching for cracks in the sand. The cracks are a sign that desert truffles are beneath, pushing up on the sand from below. People eat desert truffles in many ways: with scrambled eggs, on skewers with lamb, or in a camel milk and truffle soup, to name a few.

Truffles and other fungi are a food that people all over the world have loved to eat for thousands of years. But other kinds of fungi invoke terror . . . for even one little bite could cause severe illness or a slow, mysterious death for their unknowing victims.

Some mushrooms are so bad they give the rest of the fungi a reputation they may not deserve. Such mushrooms might look almost exactly like other safe-to-eat kinds, yet they are far from safe. They are toxic enough to kill. Even the most experienced foragers can misidentify the mushrooms they pick. That's what happened to British author Nicholas Evans, who wrote the best-selling novel *The Horse Whisperer*. He had been picking mushrooms since he was a young boy but made a near-fatal mistake one day in the Scottish countryside.

While on vacation at his in-laws' home during the summer of 2008, Evans went out to forage in a forest known for its ceps and chanterelles. It had been ten years since he'd last foraged, and Evans found what he thought were ceps, *Boletus edulis*.

He returned from the forest with a basketful, and his wife and in-laws were excited to try them. Evans fried them with butter, sprinkled them with parsley, and then he, his wife, his brother-in-law, and his sister-in-law all sat down to eat their handpicked meal. But no one had consulted the wild mushroom identification guide in their kitchen, and the next day they realized their mistake.

They woke up feeling odd, and by noon they knew they were seriously ill. They looked in the mushroom guide and found a photograph of the mushroom they ate—it looked a bit like ceps, but it had gills (which ceps does not). The mushroom they ate was instead the deadly webcap, *Cortinarius speciosissimus*, which can cause kidney, liver, and spinal cord damage. Evans's sister-in-law hadn't eaten as much as the others, so she did not suffer as badly. The other three were not as lucky. They rushed to the hospital and within a few days were vomiting blood and bile and going into kidney failure. They were fighting for their lives and needed a treatment called dialysis to filter waste, excess liquid, and toxins from their blood, which the kidneys usually handle. They survived but needed to get kidney

The deadly webcap is easily mistakable for its edible lookalike, ceps.

FUNGIPHOBIA

Some people have a phobia of accidentally eating poisonous mushrooms. That phobia is called fungiphobia, or mycophobia. Someone with fungiphobia may experience heightened anxiety or stress just at the thought of mushrooms. They may even have a panic attack. Some people with fungiphobia also avoid restaurants where mushrooms are served.

transplants. Just one deadly meal changed their lives forever, the result of toxic fungi.

THE DEADLY DEATH CAP

For as long as people have been eating mushrooms, they have been harmed by them too. So often, the deadly mushrooms look very similar to their safe and delicious cousins. Most poisonings are therefore accidental—the results of misidentification. But some poisonings have not been so innocent and instead caused with murderous intent. The biggest offender throughout history is the *Amanita phalloides*, or the death cap. Although it closely resembles straw and Caesar's mushrooms (two edible varieties), just one small piece of its cap can kill a grown person.

It's an unsuspecting mushroom—one that tastes good and shows no sign of the upcoming turmoil for its victim for at least six hours. All the while, the mushroom's toxin permeates its victim's body. Then the effects appear. First vomiting and diarrhea occur, followed by severe weakness. The victim fluctuates between the two states, sometimes for days, until dying from the fungi.

The death cap is incredibly deadly to people. But scientists have said that some animals, such as squirrels and rabbits, seem to be able to safely eat it.

Ancient Romans knew of the death cap's delayed ill effects, and some believe it's what killed Roman Emperor Claudius in 54 CE. His son from a previous marriage, Britannicus, was set to take control when Claudius died, but his wife, Agrippina, wanted her son Nero to gain power instead. Ancient historians recorded that Agrippina was likely behind a dish of poisoned mushrooms Claudius ate. The next day he was dead. The historian Suetonius wrote,

> That Claudius was poisoned is the general belief, but when it was done and by whom is disputed. Some say that it was his taster, the eunuch [a castrated man, often employed in a palace] Halotus, as he was banqueting on the Citadel with the priests; others that at a family dinner Agrippina served the drug to him with her own hand in mushrooms, a dish of which he was extravagantly fond.

FAIRYTALE TOADSTOOLS

Have you seen illustrations of mushrooms with bright red caps spotted with white dots? It's the typical fairytale mushroom, often called a toadstool. You can see these mushrooms in children's books, Renaissance paintings, and Victorian-era paintings, often with fairies or gnomes sitting atop them. This common fairytale toadstool is really the *Amanita muscaria*, or fly agaric mushroom, which has mind-altering effects. The term *toadstool* is often used to describe undesirable mushrooms.

Another historian, Tacitus, wrote about how Agrippina chose the poison she wanted to use:

> It was then that Agrippina, long since bent upon the impious [wicked] deed, and eagerly seizing the present occasion, well furnished too as she was with wicked agents, deliberated upon the nature of the poison she would use, whether, if it were sudden and instantaneous in its operation, the desperate achievement would not be brought to light: if she chose materials slow and consuming in their operation, whether Claudius, when his end approached, and perhaps having discovered the treachery, would not resume his affection for his son. Something of a subtle nature was therefore resolved upon, such as would disorder his brain and require time to kill.

The ancient Romans only knew of one poison that could cause death in this way—the death cap mushroom. It's debated whether Claudius unknowingly ate a dish of death caps or if the

A POTENTIAL ANTIDOTE

In 2023 Chinese and Australian researchers made a potential breakthrough for death cap victims. They isolated human cells and edited the cells to break their genes from the inside. Then they added amatoxins to see whether the cells survived. Cells that survived had a broken STT3B gene, so the researchers wondered if the gene was what moved the toxin into cells. They tested their theory in mice, using a common drug known to inhibit STT3B—indocyanine green (ICG), an iodide-based dye doctors use to diagnose eye diseases. The mice's survival rate increased between 20 and 50 percent, leading the team to state that "ICG has shown great potential for treating [amatoxin] poisoning in mice and ICG treatment can significantly attenuate [amatoxin]-induced damage in the liver and kidney, the two major [amatoxin]-targeting organs, resulting in improved survival." While this theory still needs to be tested in humans, it could potentially become a death cap antidote that saves people's lives.

death cap's poison was imbued within a sauce or dried death caps were sprinkled onto edible mushrooms. While we may never know exactly how Claudius was poisoned, these accounts point to the death cap being involved. And the results were what Agrippina hoped for—her son Nero took control over the mighty Roman Empire.

While Claudius may be its most famous and highly debated victim, the death cap accounts for about 90 percent of all mushroom-related deaths each year. The fungus contains a cocktail of toxins: amatoxins, phallotoxins, and virotoxins. The deadliest of the three is amatoxin. It enters the body's cells and inhibits the function of nuclear RNA polymerase II (an enzyme involved in the body's process to make proteins), which then prevents the cells from producing proteins. Ultimately, amatoxin kills the cells, and organ failure results. The liver is most affected, along with the kidneys, and many of the death cap's victims require organ transplants. About 50 percent of people who eat the mushroom die. It's best to just avoid all *Amanita* species, according to mushroom identification guides. This is a mushroom species that only a lucky few escape alive.

MORE DEADLIES

The webcap, which Nicholas Evans mistakenly picked and ate, contains the toxin orellanine. It stops the kidney's production of protein. Often, the symptoms of poisoning are delayed by several days while the toxin does bodily damage. Even then, its symptoms may seem related to the flu. Victims often need dialysis and organ transplants, as Evans did, to survive.

Other deadly mushrooms include what are called little brown mushrooms (or LBMs). One is the *Conocybe rugosa*, or fool's conecap. It contains the same deadly toxin as the death cap—amatoxin—and its victims suffer from the same ill effects. It's a woodland mushroom, often found growing on wood chips and in leaf litter. Many people dismiss its effects as food poisoning or norovirus, and the symptoms can even temporarily subside but then return to cause liver or kidney failure.

Another mushroom containing amatoxin is the *Galerina marginata*, also called the deadly galerina. Growing on conifer and broadleaf tree stumps, it's another LBM that people should avoid. Luckily, it does not look like another edible mushroom that people like to eat, so few people accidentally ingest this mushroom.

MUSHROOM IDENTIFIERS

During mushroom season, poisoning is always a risk. Poison control centers often don't know how to identify cases of mushroom poisoning, so they call on mushroom identifiers—volunteer identification consultants listed with the North American Mycological Association or known experts living near the centers. Ron Spinosa is one of the consultants in Minnesota who helps identify toxic mushrooms. He's been identifying mushrooms for more than twenty years and knows what it takes to effectively do so.

An identifier needs to educate themselves about the deadly and dangerous poisonous mushrooms in the area. He knows that in Minnesota, for example, the deadly poisonous mushrooms include these:

- destroying angel, *Amanita bisporigera*
- deadly galerina, *Galerina marginata*
- false morels, *Gyromitra*

Spinosa also knows that the dangerous poisonous mushrooms include these:

- jack-o'-lantern, *Omphalatus illudens*
- green gill, *Chlorophylum molybdites*
- fly agaric, *Amanita muscaria*
- muscarine containing mushrooms, *Clitocybe* and *Inocybe*
- orange *Cortinarius* species
- local toxic species in the genus *Agaricus*

Good identifiers must also know the symptoms of poisoning from various mushroom toxins. A sample or photographs of the mushroom in question are also essential, including both a top and bottom view. Using a sample or good photographs, knowledge of toxic mushrooms and their symptoms, and field guides as resources, the identifier can identify the mushroom to the genus level.

Many times this process has to happen quickly to save lives. Spinosa has been sent mushrooms in a taxi from an emergency room. And his work hasn't just helped people. Identification helps dogs that have been poisoned too. Volunteers such as Spinosa are critical partners to poison control centers, using their interest and knowledge of fungi to help others every year.

The destroying angels or death angels are a group of *Amanita* mushrooms—*Amanita bisporigera, Amanita virosa*, and *Amanita verna*. These white mushrooms can look a lot like the common button mushroom and meadow mushrooms. Their toxicity also comes from amatoxins.

The deadly dapperling (*Lepiota brunneoincarnata*) is a mushroom with a brown-scaled cap that grows in grassy fields. It's often mistaken for edible varieties but also contains the deadly amatoxins.

Podostroma cornu-damae, or poison fire coral, can't even be touched. Its poison can be absorbed through the skin. Fairly rare, it's usually found in Japan, Korea, and sometimes Australia. It's bright red and looks like bits of coral sticking up from the ground. It contains several kinds of trichothecene

The poison fire coral is sometimes also called the fire mushroom.

SCIENTIFIC NAMING OF SPECIES

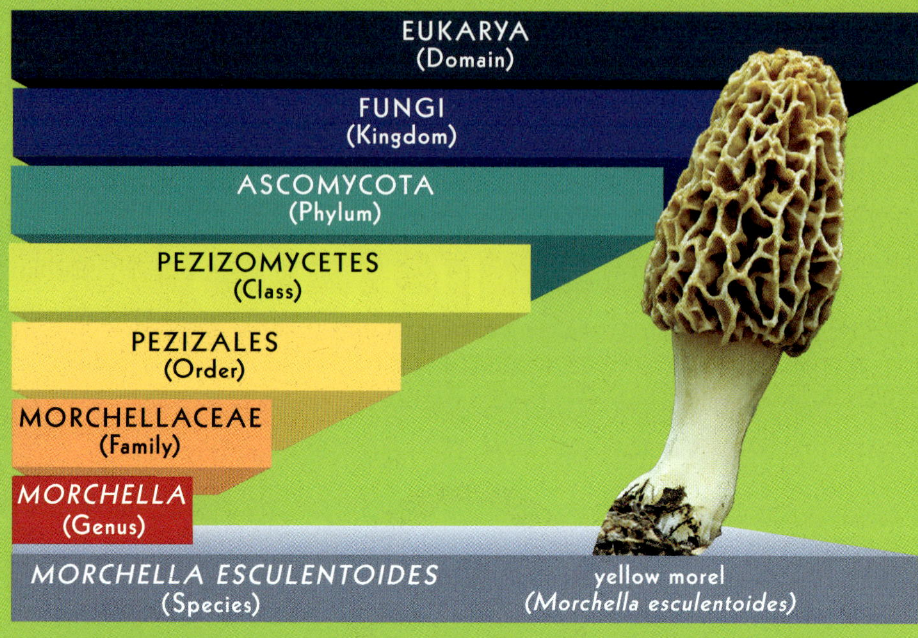

Organisms are named using a system of groups based on their characteristics. The groups go from general (at the top) to very specific (at the bottom). This is the full scientific name for the yellow morel.

mycotoxins, which can slow the body's production of proteins and nucleic acid. Touching the mushroom can cause your skin to swell and sting, but eating one causes much worse symptoms. Stomach cramps and vomiting are common, but victims may also experience peeling skin, hair loss, a shrunken brain, and loss of white blood cells and platelets. If not treated, victims may experience organ failure and die.

All these poisonous mushrooms (and others not described here) may have developed their toxicity as a defense mechanism. While some mushrooms try to lure animals to help spread their spores, these mushrooms do the opposite.

CROP KILLERS

Some fungi aren't toxic to humans but are harmful to the food humans eat. These crop killers include rust and smut fungi that infect plants and harm them. Wheat, coffee, tomatoes, beans, and corn are just a few of the crops that these fungi can destroy. More than nineteen thousand kinds of fungi harm crops each year.

Rust fungi come from the *Basidiomycota* phylum, causing plants to develop yellow, orange, red, brown, or black spots on young plants, leaves, and fruits. This causes the plants to stop growing as well as they can and sometimes die. Some of the plants rusts affect include wheat, apple trees, asparagus, and coffee plants. Rust fungi spores land on plants and then grow hyphae into the plant's tissue and cells. The fungus creates the

OUR MYCOBIOMES

You have fungi inside you and on you—we all have a mycobiome. Only a few species can survive inside humans though. They must be able to live in high temperatures, get inside our bodies, feed on human tissue, and defend themselves against our immune system. A few that can do so include the *Candida* species, *Cladosporium*, *Aureobasidium*, and *Saccharomyces boulardii*. Many fungi live in our gastrointestinal tract and are beneficial to our health. Other fungi live on our skin and can cause infections. These fungal infections can result in athlete's foot, diaper rash, ringworm, and dandruff. Some fungi are connected to pancreatic cancer too. Fungi in the *Malassezia* genus (a yeast-like variety) are often found on the head and torso. But our feet are where the most variety of fungi are—between our toes, on our nails, and on our heels. Thick and broken toenails, itchy rashes, and other kinds of discomfort ensue.

rust-colored pustules on the plant's surface, which then release spores that land on new areas on the plant, creating more rustlike spots. Some rust fungi need to infect two host plants to complete their life cycle, and some may have five spore stages.

Smut fungi also come from the *Basidiomycota* phylum and commonly affect plants in the grass family, such as corn, wheat, and barley, along with onions, grains, and other plants. Some smuts only harm a plant in the spot where they land, while others affect the entire plant. Their spores can survive in the soil through all kinds of conditions. Their hyphae enter the plant through an opening and grow in between its cells, eventually invading them. Smuts then form galls, or enlarged bumps filled with spores. When mature, the galls split open to release a large

The corn smut *Ustilago maydis* might take over the entire ear of corn as it grows.

THE LAST OF US

Imagine a world where people have suddenly become zombies. They have growths coming out of their skin, and they cannot speak or act as humans do. Just like what the zombie-ant fungus does to ants, a terrible fungus has taken control of their bodies and minds. This is the postapocalyptic world described in the hit show *The Last of Us*, based on the video game of the same name, where humans are the hosts for an invasive fungal species. The idea is based on the *Cordyceps* fungus, which infects and controls ants. But don't worry, *Cordyceps* cannot survive the high temperatures of a human body. So, humans probably won't become fungal zombies anytime soon.

mass of black or brown spores. Corn smut, called huitlacoche in Mexico, damages the plant but also makes it delicious. Some call it the Mexican truffle. People use it in sauces, tamales, and many other recipes, where it adds a smoky, savory flavor.

Farmers use fungicides and other methods to try to control fungal damage to their crops. Still, fungi manage to destroy 10 to 20 percent of crops worldwide each year, equal to losses of about $100 to $200 billion.

Deadly fungi can harm people and their food sources. But they only represent a few of the many varieties—some of which may heal people from the inside out.

Some call it the mushroom of immortality, and it's been used for thousands of years in Asia. It's thought to have many healing properties and be practically a cure-all for a wide variety of ailments—cancer, high blood pressure, respiratory issues, obesity, immune issues, and much more. All this from one fungus? Yes, reishi, also called Ling Zhi or *Ganoderma sichuanense*, is thought to be the most potent medicinal mushroom of them all.

According to Professor Masao Mori in Japan, reishi might even help with memory loss. He has been working to help dementia patients in an ambitious effort to eliminate dementia worldwide. Dementia is a debilitating terminal disease that takes away mostly older adults' memories until they no

Reishi mushrooms are thought to potentially also help reduce stress and improve sleep.

longer remember who their families are, how to do simple tasks—and even forget who they are. It has no known cure and can result in death. One study showed that elders in the Japanese community of Hisayama have a 50 percent chance of developing the disease. With an aging population and one of the highest life expectancies in the world, dementia is a critical issue in Japan. One in five people over the age of sixty-five there may develop dementia by 2025.

Mori is the president of the Dementia Improved Support Association of Japan. He's an expert in the field of microcirculation—blood flow through the circulatory system's smallest vessels, such as the capillaries and arterioles, taking oxygen to and from tissues. Studies show that people with dementia have reduced blood flow through capillaries in their brains, and the reduction increases with the severity of the dementia. So, Mori and the association developed a supplement they named Kouka. Its primary ingredient is the reishi mushroom. "The mushroom helps the circulation of capillary blood flow to the brain," said Mori. Through a clinical trial, Mori and the association distributed Kouka to early-stage dementia patients, who took the pill up to four times a day.

Kouka is also being used in the town of Ichikai, part of Japan's Orange Plan, a program to help normalize the lives of dementia patients. The town wants to help people with dementia live happy lives, and it has built an intentional community to do so. Part of the initiative is to incorporate Kouka into the residents' daily diets, and the town is working closely with Miro to see if the supplement may help. Dr. Masaru Takahashi, the president of Tokyo's Pharmaceutical Association, believes that curing dementia may involve multiple strategies and that "Kouka, paired with other cognitive exercises and other memory supplements, can be very effective in regaining memory." Even his mother, who has dementia, is taking it. He says, "Her mood has changed dramatically since taking the [Kouka]."

Time and additional clinical trials will show what Kouka and reishi's effectiveness will be in treating or preventing dementia. Just like many kinds of fungi, we need to study them more to find out. But we do know that their use in traditional medicine demonstrates that certain fungi have important medicinal qualities, which many cultures have long used to heal the body and the brain.

ANCIENT MEDICINES

Throughout history, many cultures have used mushrooms and fungi medicinally. The discovery of the mummified,

THE MIGHTY AGARIKON

Longevity is a clue that an organism has developed abilities to survive all kinds of destructive forces. If it can live long, it likely has an advanced self-defense system. Agarikon (*Fomitopsis officinalis*) has mastered longevity in the fungal world—it can live seventy-five years or more. It survives in old growth forests in Europe, Asia, and the Pacific Northwest. Greek physician Pedanius Dioscorides wrote about agarikon in 65 CE, calling it an elixir of long life and using it to treat respiratory illness and consumption (now called tuberculosis). Recent laboratory studies have shown it to have antimicrobial compounds that harm tuberculosis bacteria. Strains have also shown abilities to fight viruses such as pox, swine and bird flu, and herpes.

fifty-three-hundred-year-old Ötzi the Iceman in Italy's northern alps showed that prehistoric people likely knew about some of the healing properties of fungi. In his preserved pouch were bits of amadou, which can be used to not only start fires but also to stop bleeding, and the birch polypore *Fomitopsis betulina*, which may have antimicrobial, anticancer, and anti-inflammatory properties. Perhaps Copper Age explorers carried these fungal medicines to help them survive their long journeys. This same birch polypore has long been used as a folk medicine in eastern European countries, including Russia, Hungary, and Romania.

The ancient Greeks used certain fungi as medicine too. The physician Hippocrates lived from 460 to 375 BCE, and many consider him the originator of modern medicine. He classified the amadou mushroom as having anti-inflammatory properties and described its use to cauterize wounds. The physician would light the fungus on fire, let the flame die down, and then apply the smoldering fungus to the patient's skin to stop the bleeding. Amadou was also applied to the skin over wounds and burns to absorb fluids and used as a warm compress.

Traditional Chinese, Japanese, Russian, and Korean medicine has long included mushrooms for their many healing properties. In China these mushrooms were described in ancient books about medicinal materials. The first of these books is the *Shen Nong Ben Cao Jing* (*The Divine Husbandman's Classic of Materia Medica*), compiled between 25 to 220 CE. Some of the fungi described in the books are reishi, chaga, *Cordyceps*, turkey tail, and *Tropicoporus linteus*.

In North America, Indigenous peoples also have used mushrooms medicinally for thousands of years. One example is the puffball. Different nations have used puffballs for a variety of purposes. The Arikara use them as an ingredient in poultices. The Cherokee and Navajo use them to help heal sores and burns. Many nations use dried and powdered puffballs in wounds or broken skin to promote healing.

HEALING SCIENCE

Modern scientists research how mushrooms may heal our bodies. They are revealing that some of the most powerful medicinal effects of mushrooms are their immunity-boosting and antioxidant activities. Antioxidants may help slow the damaging aspects of aging, cardiovascular disease, cancer, and inflammatory diseases. A powerful immune system response can help us fight infections better, restore damaged bone marrow, and assist cancer-fighting treatments.

Inside fungi's cell walls may be some of its most important immunity-regulating compounds—the polysaccharide beta-glucan. Beta-glucans work with chitin to form the fungal

Puffball mushrooms are an important part of traditional Indigenous medicine in North America.

BETA-GLUCAN ABSORPTION AND TRANSPORTATION

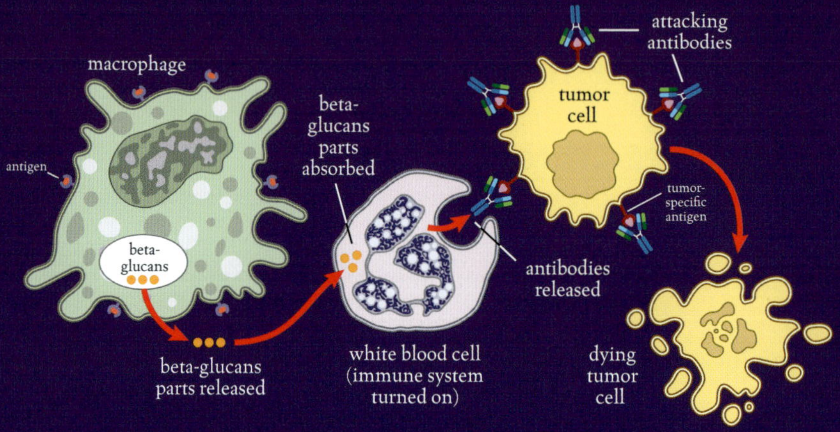

Beta-glucans are thought to work by being absorbed, broken down, and then sent in to activate white blood cells, which drive the body's immune response.

cell wall structure. To access these beta-glucans, we must first break down the cell wall by heating mushrooms before we eat them. Beta-glucans are tightly bonded with chitin, and high heat breaks those bonds, making them more soluble for our bodies.

Laboratory test tube and animal studies have demonstrated what beta-glucans can do. They pass through the digestive system intact, and then M cells in the intestinal wall absorb them. These immune system cells are like guards for the intestinal tract—they capture possible pathogens, which can infect the body and cause illness. The M cells then transport the beta-glucans to macrophages, immune system cells that break down pathogens and parts of fungal cell walls. Once the beta-glucans bind to the macrophages, they are broken down into smaller particles. Then the macrophages move to other parts of the body and release the beta-glucans, where other immune cells take them. This activates the innate immune system response from T cells, natural killer cells (which kill cancer cells or cells infected by a virus), and antibodies. Essentially, beta-glucans may turn on the immune system, making its cells ready to destroy pathogens, such as cancerous tumors.

Because of this believed immune-activating ability, fungal beta-glucans have been combined with traditional cancer treatments: chemotherapy and radiotherapy. Cancer causes cells to rapidly grow out of control, forming tumors that take over parts of the body and stop its regular function. Cancer itself can weaken the immune system by spreading into bone marrow, where infection-fighting B and T cells are made. B cells make antibodies that lock onto germs, damaged cells, and harmful invaders, marking them for destruction. T cells either help B cells make antibodies or attack the body's damaged and sickened cells. Chemotherapy and radiotherapy also temporarily weaken the immune system. Chemotherapy targets fast-growing cells and kills them, which can damage bone marrow cells and cause them to stop producing B and T cells. The radiation used in radiotherapy damages cellular genetic material, which kills both cancer cells and B and T cells. Using beta-glucans during these treatments may boost the immune system's effectiveness, helping patients fight tumors and any harmful bacteria or viruses that enter their body during cancer treatment.

One of the first scientific studies of a mushroom's antitumor activities was published in 1957. Scientists used an extract of *Boletus edulis* (often called the king bolete or penny-bun bolete) to successfully treat mice with sarcoma, a cancer of the bone marrow or soft tissues. Since then, many clinical studies have focused on the anticancer properties of various fungi. An extract from turkey tail (*Trametes versicolor*) called polysaccharide-K (PSK) has shown to be effective in treating cancer and was developed in Japan. Clinical studies using

TOP BETA-GLUCAN COUNTS

Every mushroom has beta-glucans, but not all beta-glucan counts are the same. Some species have fairly low counts, while others are packed with beta-glucans. White button mushrooms have low percentages: 8.6 percent of the cap and 12.3 percent of the stalk per 3.5 ounces (100 g) of dry matter. Compare that with the mushrooms in this table that have some of the highest beta-glucan counts.

SPECIES	DRY MATTER PER 100 G (%)
Turkey tail (*Trametes versicolor*)	60.8
Reishi (*Ganoderma* species)	54
Sulphur shelf/chicken of the woods (*Laetiporus sulphureus*)	47
Jelly rot (*Phlebia tremellosa*, formerly *Merulius tremellosus*)	53.5
Birch Polypore (*Fomitopsis betulina*, formerly *Piptoporus betulinus*)	51.8

PSK have shown positive results and better survival rates for patients with gastric and colon cancer and may also help with esophageal cancer. Another extract from turkey tail, polysaccharide-peptide (PSP), was later developed in China. A study with PSP in addition to chemotherapy showed that it slowed the progression of non-small cell lung cancer. Other PSP trials have shown effectiveness in treating stomach, esophageal, and gynecological cancers. Many beta-glucan trials such as these have occurred in China and Japan. As of 2024, a few US clinical trials testing the effectiveness of beta-glucans in combination with other cancer therapies are underway for patients with neuroblastoma, a cancer of immature nerve tissue.

MORE BENEFICIAL COMPOUNDS

Not as well studied as fungal beta-glucans are compounds that have antioxidant, anti-inflammatory, and other beneficial properties: terpenes and phenolic compounds. Terpenes are aromatic compounds made from hydrocarbons and found in both fungi and plants. In nature, they can attract pollinators, repel predators, or work within an organism's immune system to protect it from infections. Diterpenes and triterpenes are two kinds that researchers have studied for their healthful effects.

Lion's mane and reishi have diterpenes and triterpenes associated with a variety of beneficial biological activities. Some laboratory and animal studies show they can slow leukemia and prostate cancer cell growth. Studies involving cells and mice have shown promise for the compounds' nerve-regenerating effects in the brain. This could be beneficial in the treatment of Alzheimer's disease, which results from nerve damage and the loss of connections in the brain. Terpenes have strong antibiotic qualities too. One (erinacine) has shown effectiveness in battling the Methicillin-resistant Staphylococcus aureus (MRSA) bacteria.

Fungi also contain phenolic compounds, some of which have strong antioxidant properties. The compounds capture free radicals—unstable atoms that can damage cells in the body and cause people to age faster or become ill. Many fungi have antioxidant properties that researchers are only beginning to study. These fungi could have antiaging effects, help reduce cardiovascular disease, prevent cancer, boost the immune system, and reduce inflammatory diseases.

MODERN MEDICINES

While traditional medicine has long used fungi mostly to support good health and as a preventative measure for various ailments, modern medicine has developed specialized medications from fungi for certain uses and in response to illnesses. Perhaps one of the most well known of these medications is the antibiotic penicillin, which a *Penicillium* fungus makes naturally. *Penicillium* is a common blue-green mold that can grow pretty much anywhere—from soil to plants to the air—and decomposes organic material. It also has an important defense against bacteria—it exudes a compound that destroys them by making their cell walls explode. This compound is penicillin, and some say its discovery brought medicine into the modern age.

Before penicillin was discovered, a minor infection from a cut could result in death. We had few ways to combat infections. So, in 1928 Alexander Fleming's accidental discovery of penicillin's medical potential was a scientific breakthrough. The Scottish bacteriologist had been studying *Staphylococcus* bacteria (which is commonly found in people's noses or on their skin and can cause a range of infections) in London. The bacteria were growing in petri dishes in his laboratory, which he left while he went on a vacation. When Fleming returned, he noticed something odd had happened in his absence. Mold had started growing in some of the dishes along with the bacteria cultures, and it seemed to stop the bacteria from growing. He

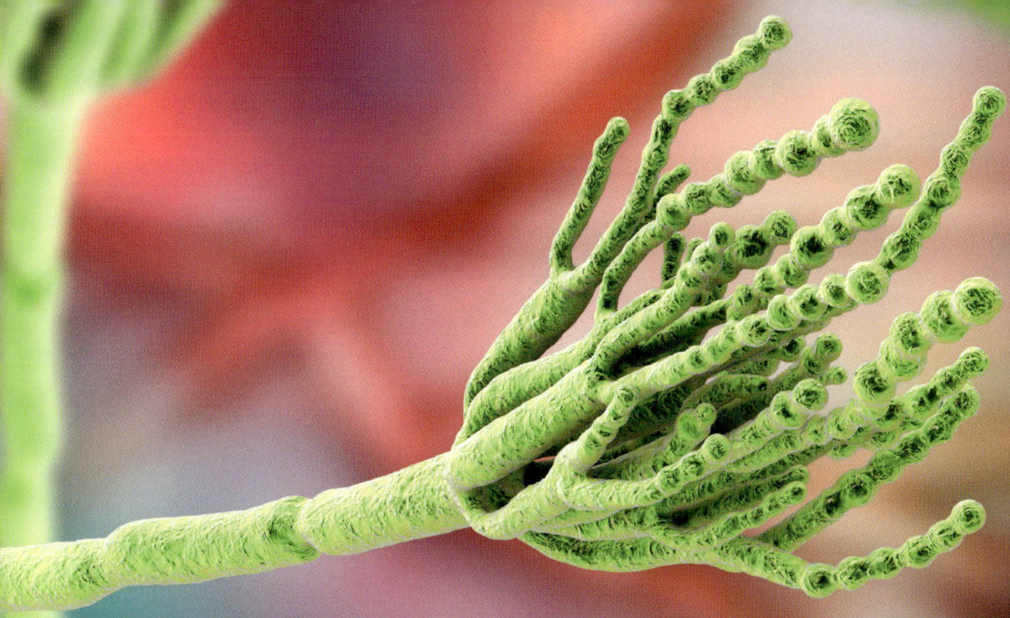

Like other molds, *Penicillium* reproduces by growing spores at the tips of its hyphae and releasing them.

isolated a compound that the mold made and saw that it killed many kinds of bacteria that harmed humans. In the 1930s, two other scientists—Howard Florey and Ernst Chain—further developed the compound by isolating and purifying it from the original mold. They first tested it on mice, and by the early 1940s, it was ready for human use as an injectable medicine.

There was a problem, though—the scientists did not know how to produce enough of penicillin to do any good for patients in need. In 1941 US pharmaceutical development of penicillin began at a laboratory in Peoria, Illinois. Researchers there were experienced with large-scale fermentation and had an excess of corn steep liquor (a by-product of corn products). And then in 1943 Mary Hunt, a lab assistant, found an even better *Penicillium* mold to use growing on a rotten cantaloupe at a local market. The corn steep liquor proved to be an excellent medium to quickly grow the new strain of the mold, which produced six times the amount of penicillin that

MOLDY MEDICINE

People around the world used mold as medicine long before Alexander Fleming's discovery. Here's how some people used mold pre-penicillin:

- Australian First Nations peoples scraped mold off the shaded side of eucalyptus trees and treated wounds with it.
- The Jewish Talmud, a text of ancient Jewish teachings, refers to kutach bayli, or chamka, a moldy cure made of what was translated as corn (but could also mean a kind of grain) soaked in date wine.
- From 1500 BCE, an ancient Egyptian medical text called the Papyrus Hearst refers to illnesses that can be cured with mold.
- English writings from 1640 and 1760 CE suggest using moldy bread and other molds to treat wounds.

Fleming's strain did. Pharmaceutical companies then started producing this penicillin on a large scale, and the antibiotic was one of the drugs that helped save many lives of Allied forces during World War II (1939–1945). Since major Axis powers Japan and Germany did not yet have this medicine, it may have helped the Allies win the war. This powerful antibiotic continues to save lives.

Since the commercial production of penicillin began, scientists have developed other important medications from fungi. These medications can help our bodies resist fungal diseases, better accept transplanted tissues and organs, and reduce cholesterol. Micafungin is a medicine used to treat the fungal infections candidiasis and candidemia and is derived from a fungus called *Coleophoma empetri* that rots cranberries and other plants. Cyclosporine A comes from the *Tolypocladium inflatum* fungus, and it has anti-inflammatory, immune system repression, antifungal, and antiparasitic qualities. This medication is used to help the body accept transplanted bone marrow, kidneys, hearts, and livers. A big risk with transplants is the body's immune system, which often attacks transplanted tissues and organs, seeing them as harmful invaders. Similarly, mycophenolate suppresses the immune system and helps prevent transplanted organ and tissue rejection. It is also used to treat autoimmune disorders, such as Crohn's disease. This medication was developed from certain *Penicillium* strains, especially *Penicillium brevicompactum*. Lovastatin is another helpful medication, first developed from the *Aspergillus terreus* fungus, that can help lower cholesterol in our blood and treat and prevent heart disease.

Fungi are often harmed by the same bacteria and microbes that affect humans, so their defense systems can help us too. This is what makes many fungi ideal sources for new medications. With many fungi yet to be discovered and studied, a wealth of potential medicines may be growing all around us. They may not only heal our bodies and prevent illnesses but also be key to healing our minds.

CHAPTER 7

THE MIND CHANGERS

Hearing that you have cancer can lead your mind into a dark place. When Dr. Pradeep Bansal learned he had cancer, it was unexpected and a complete jolt to his life. The first sign that something was wrong was blood in his urine. Next, doctors found stage I cancer in his kidney, and after successful treatment, Bansal thought the worst was over. But then he learned it had spread to his lung and his bladder, and he had stage IV cancer. As a doctor, Bansal knew the implications: His prospects were not good, and he might die soon. He sought the painful but necessary physical treatment for the disease, but he was suffering emotionally too. It was a lot to take.

"My world just fell apart," Bansal said. "All the golden and wonderful years of life I had expected to live up to and was looking forward to, that all became a very dim and dark future." Bansal could not sleep, he lacked energy, he didn't want to do anything fun, and he was very emotional. He felt he had fallen into a deep depression. He had a loving wife of forty years, two grown children, and was awaiting the birth of his first grandchild. He had so much to live for, yet he realized, "Suddenly, I wasn't sure I was going to last that long." Whatever time he had left he did not want to spend in constant worry. But what could he do?

Bansal saw a therapist and tried seeking solace in meditation. He also exercised and focused on positive thoughts. But nothing eased his debilitating depression. He was skeptical about alternative therapies, though. "I don't have much patience for holistic medicine, homeopathy, acupuncture, or alternative medicines with claims of spiritual upliftment or altered states of mind," he said. He wanted the scientific evidence first, and he had read some promising results from clinical trials using psilocybin-assisted therapies. Psilocybin—a chemical made by more than two hundred kinds of fungi—is known to produce mind-altering effects in people.

Along with psychological therapy, some clinical studies have tested psilocybin's effectiveness in treating major depressive disorder. Bansal saw positive results of several small clinical trials involving people with late-stage cancer and related anxiety and depression—they experienced significantly less depression and anxiety twelve months after treatment. One 2016 Johns Hopkins University study even showed that after a single large dose provided to participants in a controlled setting with clinically trained monitors, 80 percent of participants had significant decreases in anxiety and depression six months after treatment, and the same was true for 60 percent twelve months after treatment. Many in the study said it was one of the most significant or spiritual experiences of their lives.

More than one hundred fungi species worldwide contain psilocybin.

These results convinced Bansal that this psilocybin-assisted therapy was worth trying. After going through extensive mental health and physical screening, he was selected to participate in a trial using a large dose of a synthetic form of psilocybin called COMP360, which is produced in a laboratory. Doctors prepared him for his treatment so that he would have the right mindset going into it and feel comfortable in the setting where it was provided. He attended therapy sessions where they discussed what could happen and how to deal with any strong emotions. Bansal also got to know his personal guide through the treatment—a military psychiatrist with years of experience.

On treatment day, Bansal was taken to the dosing room with his guide. It was comfortable, more like a living room than a hospital room. He took his dose of psilocybin, put on a sleeping mask to block out the light, laid down on a couch, and put on headphones to hear soothing music and birdsongs. For the next seven and a half hours, Bansal experienced the psychedelic effects of the psilocybin—seeing images and colors and going through an experience within his mind, all the while knowing that his guide was there if he needed him. He saw something he felt represented his cancer, and it scared him. But his guide told him to face it, and he did. Then the image disappeared, and he felt a deep sense of calm. It made Bansal feel as if the cancer was not something to be so afraid of—that his cancer was one small part of his life that he could overcome. He later wrote in his journal, "It seems that as time is passing on, I'm becoming more relaxed and hopeful, more calm, and at peace." And while Bansal still felt the physical pain from dealing with cancer, the psilocybin-assisted therapy left him more mentally able to deal with it and go on living meaningfully.

This experience happened through modern medicine and a clinical study, helping Bansal change his thinking and overcome much of his anxiety and depression. But while modern researchers are only beginning to scientifically understand what psilocybin may do inside the brain, many American Indigenous cultures were the first to explore its effects.

INDIGENOUS KNOWLEDGE

Sacred and ancient traditions involving mushrooms of the *Psilocybe* genus that produce psilocybin have been practiced in Mesoamerican cultures for hundreds (and possibly thousands) of years. The Aztecs so revered these mushrooms that they called them Teonanácatl, meaning "divine flesh" or "flesh of the gods," and only used them for their holiest ceremonies. Knowledge of psilocybin mushrooms has been passed through generations, and Mexican ethnic groups including the Chatin, Chinantec, Matlatzinca, Mazatec, Mixe, Nahuatl, Purépecha, Totonac, and Zapotec still use the mushrooms ceremonially.

The earliest evidence of ritualistic psilocybin ceremonies comes from Mesoamerica in the Codex Yuta Tnoho (or

The Codex Yuta Tnoho explains the culture and origins of the Mixtec people.

Vindobonensis Mexicanus I) from the early 1500s CE. It is a folded, painted manuscript filled with pictures telling the story of the Mixtec people's origins, lineage, and history. On pages 24 and 25, this codex (ancient book) has been interpreted to explain a story of deities involved in a nighttime ritual with mushrooms, receiving a message for how to form a good kingdom, and then appearing changed after the sun rises for the first time.

Earlier evidence shows that the Maya culture valued mushrooms too, although the Mixtec codex is the first to connect them with a ceremony. This evidence is in the form of mushroom stones—stone sculptures carved to look like mushroom people—which have been found in Guatemala and Mexico. Hundreds of these statues have been discovered, dating back to three thousand years ago. It's possible that the Maya used them ceremonially in rituals involving the

PSILOCYBIN PETROGLYPHS?

In the Sahara Desert on the Tassili n'Ajjer plateau in Algeria are paintings dating back seven thousand to nine thousand years. One interpretation of the paintings is that they show people holding mushrooms. These mushroomlike forms are growing all around the edges of some of their bodies. The people look as though they're dancing in some sort of ritual. What could these paintings have meant to Neolithic people? Were they showing a psilocybin ritual on the cave walls? During that time, people were just starting to settle down from their hunting-and-gathering lifestyles by farming in permanent communities. Perhaps they had shamans leading psilocybin rituals too.

consumption of mushrooms containing psilocybin.

As the Spanish invaded Central America and colonized its land, people, and culture in the early 1500s, they suppressed many Indigenous practices, including the ceremonial use of psilocybin mushrooms. They did not understand or care about the significance of mushrooms to Indigenous traditions and religion, saw its effects as mere intoxication, and believed the ceremonies to be idolatry—worshipping other gods instead of their Christian God. So, they forced the Aztecs to stop openly practicing these rituals, but these rituals secretly endured and continue to be practiced today.

Western scientists and observers first widely found out about this ritual and its use of mushrooms in the 1950s, although scientific research into these hallucinogenic mushrooms occurred in the late 1930s. Botanist Richard Evans Schultes had read Spanish accounts of the mushrooms and visited northeastern Oaxaca in Mexico to find them. He brought them back to his laboratory to study them and later published his findings, saying that the mushrooms produced visions. American businessperson and amateur mycologist Gordon Wasson had read Schultes's report, went to Oaxaca to find the mushrooms, and was allowed to be the first non-Indigenous person to participate in the mushroom ritual. He was guided by the shaman María Sabina, who asked him to keep her identity private. She took him through the nighttime ritual meant to solve a physical or spiritual problem. It was solemn and held in a place free from distractions. After they all consumed the mushrooms, the shaman chanted and clapped as the psilocybin took effect, and the ceremony continued until the early hours of the morning. The mystical experience deeply affected Wasson, who broke his promise to Sabina and wrote about her and the ceremony in a 1957 *Life* magazine article that widely spread across the Western world.

These rituals still occur within some Indigenous groups. According to a report for the Oregon Psilocybin Advisory Board, which was coauthored by Uehling, modern Indigenous rituals are

> used to treat both spiritual and physical illness. *Psilocybe* mushrooms induce hallucinations and synesthesia resulting in a trancelike experience that is thought to allow dissociation of the soul from the body. As a result, bodily ailment diagnoses, introspection, self-healing, and revelation of lost persons' locations can be facilitated by traditional doctors or shamans. While practices vary between Indigenous groups, in general, ceremonies are always done with care at night in a quiet place guided by an elder or shaman, no meals, alcohol, medicine or drugs are taken in advance, and travel is discouraged for a week after.

CRIMINALIZING PSILOCYBIN

After the *Life* article, Western culture became more and more interested in psilocybin. In the late 1950s and early 1960s, research into its possible therapeutic uses occurred with thousands of patients. In 1958 Dr. Albert Hoffman was the first to characterize the mushrooms' active components as psilocybin and psilocin. The chemical seemed to help people overcome mood disorders and alcohol abuse when used with psychotherapy. Some people were also using the chemical recreationally, without a focus on healing and its therapeutic effects. Others thought that it was being abused, along with other substances, and that it was harming society.

In response, the US government criminalized psilocybin as a Schedule I drug under the Controlled Substances Act, a federal law that took effect in 1971, the same year President Richard Nixon declared a "war on drugs." A Schedule I drug is the highest classification of drugs under the law, considered to be addictive and dangerous, and this classification declared psilocybin had no medical purpose. The law made it illegal for people to use psilocybin recreationally in the United States and effectively stopped all government-funded scientific research of its therapeutic potential for the next twenty years.

In the 1990s and early 2000s, some psilocybin research with human subjects resumed as attitudes began shifting about its therapeutic potential. Then, in 2018 and 2019, the US Food and Drug Administration (FDA) designated psilocybin as a breakthrough therapy for helping people with depression. This designation accelerates a drug's pathway to medical approval within the administration. More small phase I and II clinical trials began, and as of 2024, psilocybin-assisted therapy is being tested through clinical trials at reputable institutions such as Yale, Johns

Hopkins University, New York University, and Imperial College London. In October 2021 the US government's National Institutes of Health granted Johns Hopkins Medicine the first federal grant in fifty years to fund research into the use of psilocybin-assisted therapy to treat tobacco addiction. Since then, the government has funded more studies researching psilocybin.

While psilocybin is still illegal by federal law, its medical use has been decriminalized in two states and some municipalities. Oregon has a state-regulated psilocybin therapy program and opened its first licensed psilocybin service center in September 2023. This state program received guidance from the Oregon Psilocybin Advisory Board, which gathered and presented evidence about psilocybin's use by Indigenous cultures and results of scientific research, and also offered recommendations for state requirements, specifications, and guidelines for providing psilocybin services. Colorado started a similar process in 2022, determining how psilocybin therapy centers might work in the state. And while "peer reviewed, western, scientific literature and clinical trials for psilocybin are scarce," said Uehling, a mycologist on the Oregon Psilocybin Advisory Board, "so far there is evidence in these models that psilocybin is efficacious [effective] in treating depression; anxiety disorders including end of life fears and concerns; obsessive-compulsive disorder (OCD); trauma-related disorders, including racial trauma; substance use disorders; palliative care; and more recently eating disorders."

PSILOCYBIN IN THE BRAIN

What we do know so far is that psilocybin initiates an emotional and physical experience—one that is somehow transformative to the patient. It works inside the brain, but exactly what is happening

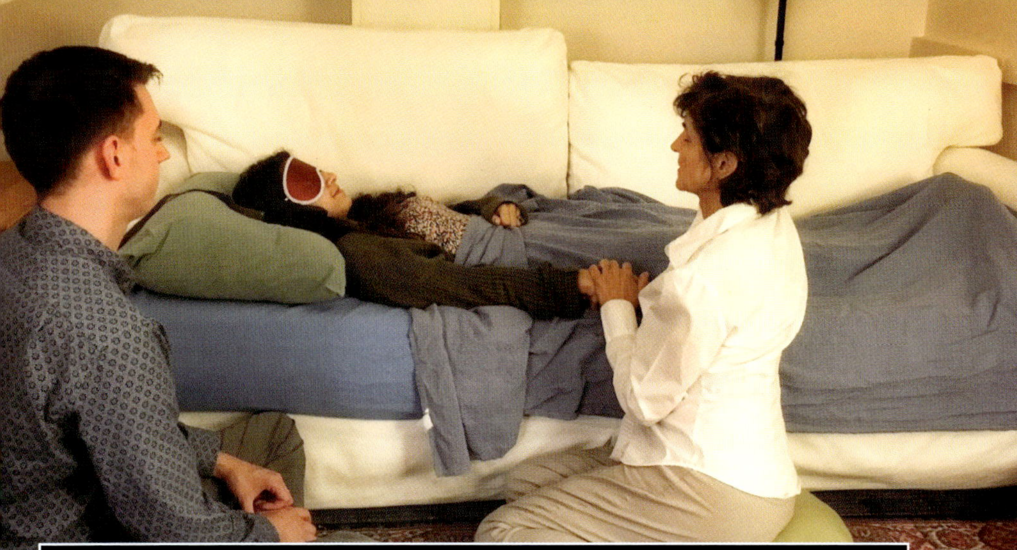

A person undergoes psilocybin-assisted treatment. Administrators try to keep the treatment rooms comfortable for their patients.

is still being discovered. Scientists know a few things though and are exploring different ways to better understand the chemical.

"On a biological level, psychedelics like psilocybin appear to bind to and activate the serotonin-2A (5-HT2A) receptor in brain cells, known to be involved with regulating mood, among many other functions," says Dr. Natalie Gukasyan, a Johns Hopkins investigator and clinician who's worked on a handful of clinical trials studying psilocybin-assisted therapy for mood and eating disorders. Brain receptors transmit chemical signals between brain cells to allow us to think, feel, and behave. The 5-HT2A receptors are typically activated by the body's own serotonin, a chemical that can be low in people who have depression or other mood disorders.

"One level up, this has an effect on how different regions of the brain communicate with one another. It can result in differences in how a person perceives things including the environment around them, or their inner experience (like emotions)," Gukasyan explained. It can make a person believe things are more or less meaningful than they normally seem.

CONNECTING MYCOLOGY WITH MENTAL HEALTH

Uehling was drawn to fungi before her psilocybin work, becoming a professor in the Department of Botany and Plant Pathology and running a mycological research lab at Oregon State University. A personal experience later brought her toward her work with psilocybin: "I lost my sister tragically when I was 20. She struggled with mental health and ended her life after a long battle with poor mental health resources in a rural area. As a result, I have always been interested in tools to gain self-awareness and improve mental health. I have always loved fungi, so the psilocybin work merged two of my passions and gave me a way to meaningfully contribute to the world."

They might hear music in a different way, and their environment could look different. "Whether and how this results in changes in mood and other outcomes is still a bit of a mystery," she says.

Psilocybin may also reopen something called a critical period, which is "a special window of time when your brain is really good at learning something specific. For example, you know how little kids seem to pick up new languages really quickly? That's because their brains are in a critical period for learning languages," says Gukasyan. "This might be important for how we think of psilocybin's effect in mental health issues because in many cases, these conditions are associated with very deeply entrenched ways of thinking and behaving, and psilocybin might make it easier to change those patterns." Researchers think this temporary window allows a person's brain to adapt and grow and maybe reassess meanings of events or change negative thought patterns.

CLINICAL TRIALS

Researchers continue to examine how psilocybin works in the brain and how it affects different disorders. It is an exciting and promising area of research with many small clinical trials ongoing. According to ClinicalTrials.gov, more than 160 clinical research trials with psilocybin were either underway or completed in early 2024. In these trials, researchers test psilocybin's effects on behaviors, such as substance use disorders, obsessive-compulsive disorder, anxiety, depression, post-traumatic stress disorder, and eating disorders. Other studies are looking at what psilocybin does biologically inside the brain and body—investigating, for example, how the body best absorbs it, how it affects brain activity, and which brain mechanisms affect visual perception.

The goal of these and future trials is to understand how effective psilocybin is in treating various disorders, how safe it is for the general public to use medically, and whether it is an addictive substance. These trials are still in their infancy and focus on small groups of people, and Gukasyan believes that "it probably will not be at least for another few years that regulatory agencies like the Food and Drug Administration decide whether the treatment is safe and effective enough to offer to the general public based on the results of that research."

Current psilocybin-assisted therapy involves intensive screening of participants, preparation for the sessions, and guiding therapists. Screening potential study participants is essential—some people are at a higher risk of serious side effects. "Serious risks can occur in those who have a personal history or family history of certain mental health issues like schizophrenia or bipolar disorder," says Gukasyan. "Sometimes, these conditions may have been undiagnosed, so people might

DR. NATALIE GUKASYAN: PATHWAY TO PSILOCYBIN RESEARCH

In her middle school's specialized science track, the future Dr. Natalie Gukasyan (*right*) was inspired to be curious about the natural world. Her middle school teacher Mr. Giamportone was a big part of that. "He taught me some fundamentals in critical thinking and public speaking, and ignited my curiosity for science—about what we do and don't know about our universe, and biology more specifically," Gukasyan said. "We did a variety of science projects for that class and even had the opportunity to design our own experiments with fruit flies."

As she continued her education, she completed a bachelor of science degree in human biology, health, and society at Cornell University in Ithaca, New York. There she read a few "interesting research papers showing that psilocybin seems to be able to produce very profound experiences in people, and that these experiences were associated with long term benefits in a variety of ways. I had wondered whether we could harness this effect to help people with different kinds of health issues. I was also intrigued by the content

not even be aware that they or their family members may have had such problems. In fact, in my clinical practice, I have treated multiple people for whom a psychedelic drug like psilocybin seemed to be the cause of their first very serious mental health issue like psychosis."

While risks exist, Gukasyan is seeing some positive results in her trial on how psilocybin-assisted therapy helps people with the eating disorder anorexia nervosa. The research team is still writing the results of their study. But she explains, "In short, we found that after two to four doses of psilocybin of the experiences themselves and how they might be produced by a drug." She explained, "I thought it might be nice to do that kind of research eventually, but thought it was a bit of a pipe dream because it had been so taboo at the time. But I was fortunate to end up at the right place at the right time."

After college she thought about becoming a surgeon and attended medical school but eventually realized that she enjoyed psychiatry much more. She was drawn to psilocybin research especially. "I did my psychiatry residency at Johns Hopkins, which was home to a world-renowned group doing research in psychedelics," Gukasyan said. "It took a few tries, but I eventually got my foot in the door and began working with and learning from them."

Today, Gukasyan is an assistant professor at Columbia University Medical Center/New York State Psychiatric Institute and an affiliate investigator at Johns Hopkins Center for Psychedelic and Consciousness Research. Her research focuses on psilocybin-assisted psychotherapy for mood, addictive, and eating disorders. Working on research has some challenges—it requires putting a lot of effort into something that may not work out and can also involve a lot of grant applications or publication rejections. "But it's exhilarating to discover something new and contribute meaningfully to open questions and debates," she says. "And while the clinical part of my job can be emotionally intense and challenging on hard days, on the good days you get to see people get better and become the best possible versions of themselves, which is very rewarding."

given in a program of psychotherapy, there were significant improvements in severity of eating disorder symptoms, as well as mood and quality of life."

Therapy is key to seeing positive results in psilocybin-assisted treatment of mental health disorders in Western medicine. Psilocybin is not a cure-all for people's problems, but it is showing potential to help under the right conditions. Larger clinical trials in the next few years may show whether it is a safe and long-lasting treatment for people with mental health disorders.

CHAPTER 8

FOREST CONNECTORS

Look up in a forest and you'll see tree crowns reaching high and wide, some bigger than others, grabbing precious sunlight where they can find it. The biggest trees have the most reach, able to produce more food through photosynthesis. They grow bigger and stronger while smaller trees below take what sunlight they can, but their size limits them. It may seem as if the trees are competing with one another, with the largest trees winning every day. But are they? If you look down at the cool and shady forest floor, you might discover a different story of the forest—one of collaboration and connection, one we are only just beginning to understand.

Tucked away in shady areas, usually near beech trees, a strange little plant reveals some of that hidden forest world.

The ghost pipe grows in many woodland regions, such as California's Redwood National and State Parks.

Completely white or tinged pink, it's not at all like the other plants there. It lacks chlorophyll, the pigment plants use for photosynthesis, so has long lost the ability to turn sunlight into food. It grows in small groups; each one has a single stem that reaches up to a single flower bent down like the end of a pipe. Its leaves are just small scales branching off from its stem, no longer necessary to its biological function. This unusual plant is the ghost pipe (*Monotropa uniflora*), and understanding how it could possibly grow opened a door into a forest's underground workings.

This small and ghostly woodland flower bewildered botanists for years. How did it get its nutrients? Did it somehow get its food like fungi, from decomposing leaves and plants? Or did it tap into tree roots? In 1819 biologist George Graves answered one of those questions after studying *Monotropa*'s roots and determining that they did not directly connect to tree roots. Then, in the 1880s, Russian botanist Franz Kamieński found another piece of evidence. He studied *Monotropa*'s roots under a microscope and saw that they were covered with hyphae. He also saw that the same hyphae covered fine tree

A POEM FOR THE GHOST PIPE

Considered one of America's greatest poets, Emily Dickinson often wrote about science and nature, and was particularly interested in plants and flowers. Born in 1830, she first made an herbarium as a teenager, a book where she preserved 424 kinds of flowers from the Amherst, Massachusetts, region. She also wrote poetry about all that she thought and observed, but the world didn't get to read her poems until four years after her death in 1886. Her first book of poetry was published in 1890, featuring a drawing of her favorite flower on the cover. The flower, which she included in her herbarium, was the ethereal ghost pipe, also called the Indian pipe. Dickinson also wrote about her favorite fungi-dependent flower. The poem, written in 1879, goes:

> 'Tis whiter than an Indian Pipe—
> 'Tis dimmer than a Lace—
> No stature has it, like a Fog
> When you approach the place—
> Not any voice imply it here—
> Or intimate it there—
> A spirit—how doth it accost—
> What function hath the Air?
> This limitless Hyperbole
> Each one of us shall be—
> 'Tis Drama— if Hypothesis
> It be not Tragedy—

roots. He then theorized that a fungus connected *Monotropa* to trees and served as its nutrient pathway.

It was a radical idea and not one that caught on—it simply faded into history until 1960. That's when scientific evidence demonstrated Kamieński's theory. The evidence came from

Swedish botanist Erik Björkman, who wanted to see if nutrients moved between trees and *Monotropa* plants. He injected trees with sugars that contained the radioactive carbon-14 isotope, which is also used to determine the age of fossils, dead animals, and other organic material. Through his study, Björkman showed that the carbon-14 accumulated in *Monotropa* plants growing nearby. So, it was clear that nutrients flowed from trees to the ghost pipe plant. And it was the photosynthesis of trees that kept the plant alive, most likely with a fungus as the delivery system.

This understanding led to other questions. What else might plants share through fungi? Could fungi connect an entire forest? And what would a fungal forest network look like? Perhaps the real story of forests was underground, and fungi were a much bigger part of it than anyone had thought before.

THE FUNGAL-TREE CONNECTION

Approximately 90 percent of all plants on land rely on their fungal relationships to survive. These relationships occur in all kinds of forests—ones in the alpine zone where coniferous trees such as pine or spruce dominate; those in the boreal zone where there's more variety, including coniferous trees and deciduous trees such as birch, oak, and trembling aspen; and tropical forests, where an incredible amount of diversity exists and trees include the Brazil nut, kapok, rubber, and many more. In all these forests, fungal-tree relationships differ though, as not all mycorrhizal fungi partner with tree roots in the same way. But these relationships are all mutually beneficial.

Two main types of fungal-tree relationships exist: ectomycorrhiza (EM) and arbuscular mycorrhiza (AM). Each uses a different kind of symbiotic interface to interact with their

MASS ORCHIDELIRIUM

During the Victorian era (1837–1901), the European elite wanted orchids from the faraway tropics. They paid exorbitant prices for the rare and beautiful treasures and built ornate greenhouses just for them. They even hired orchid hunters to go on expeditions to find this elusive prize because owning orchids meant you were a person of means and culture. But there was a slight problem—these very expensive orchids were nearly impossible to grow from seed. To get another meant another costly expedition to find a grown plant. This puzzled botanists; even with moisture, humidity, and warm temperatures, the seeds would not germinate. Soon they discovered that something unexpected was missing. The orchids needed certain fungi to survive. Botanists at the time thought that the fungi attacked orchids, acting as parasites. But in the early 1900s, French scientist Noël Bernard published his study showing that orchids needed the fungi to live. Without the fungi, their seeds would not sprout. With this discovery, horticulturalists were able to grow orchids from seed more reliably in soil containing the fungi.

host plant. EM fungi partner with about 60 percent of trees worldwide, found in many forests around the world, but only with certain species. They partner with trees in the pine family and beech family, among others, and in some tropical areas. They can live independently of trees or bond with tree roots. To bond, their hyphae grow around tree roots, creating a thick outer shield. Then the hyphae grow just under the roots' surface into and between epidermal cells, making the Hartig net. This net is the primary site for their nutrient exchange.

AM fungi interact with tree roots in a much different way and are less picky about their hosts—about 80 percent of all land plants can partner with AM fungi. They invade the roots

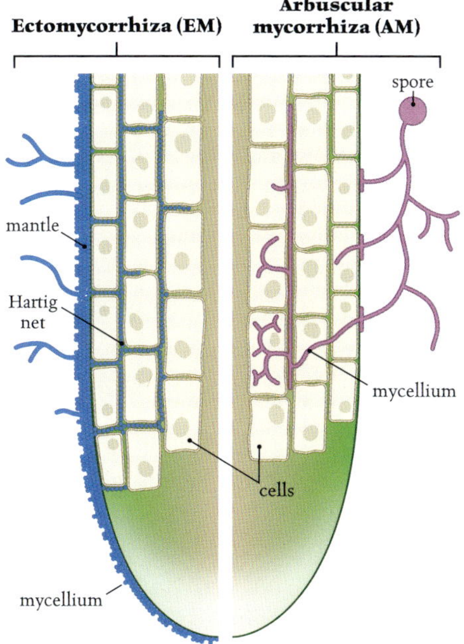

and enter the cells. First a spore grows near the tree root's surface and sends out exploratory hyphae. The hyphae penetrate the root wall and enter the tree's cells. Inside the cells, the fungi form treelike structures, called arbuscules, which serve as nutrient exchange hubs.

Both kinds of fungi help their hosts thrive and survive times of stress, such as a drought, by transporting and storing nutrients and water. Nutrients are not evenly distributed in the soil, so fungi's long-reaching mycelium can find nutrient-rich areas and deliver the nutrients to nearby trees. The two types of fungi gather nutrients differently though. AM fungi find nutrients released by microbes in the soil, while EM fungi decompose organic material in the soil. Fungi also help protect trees from diseases and harmful organisms in the soil by excreting enzymes that kill them. In return for nutrients, water, and protection, fungi receive carbohydrates and other nutrients from the trees.

A WOOD WIDE WEB

Scientists thought fungi connected with tree roots and nutrients passed from tree to tree, yet no one had actually seen that transfer happen—not until the pioneering work of United Kingdom botanist David Read. He designed a laboratory experiment to understand if those mycorrhizal connections transferred carbon and published a paper on his findings in 1984. For his experiment, Read created observation chambers in which he planted pine seedlings whose roots were connected to fungi. Next to them, Read planted younger seedlings not connected to the fungi. Soon, the fungi had grown from the older seedlings and attached to the roots of the younger seedlings. Then Read covered the older seedlings from the soil up inside a clear box and exposed them to radioactive carbon dioxide. Some of the younger seedlings were also shaded from light.

Using autoradiographs (photography that can detect radioactive decay from radioactive carbon dioxide), Read saw the carbon dioxide in the older seedling's roots, the connected mycelium, and the younger seedling's roots. He also found that shaded seedlings received more carbon from the older seedling than unshaded ones did. These autoradiographs proved that carbon could transfer between seedlings through fungal mycelium. But while this was a big advance in scientific understanding of mycorrhizal function, the experiment took place in the controlled conditions of a laboratory. Could the same be proved out in a forest?

Dr. Suzanne Simard was the researcher to find out. In 1997 she published her study of birch, fir, and cedar tree seedlings in a forest. She wanted to test carbon transfer between trees, so she exposed pairs of trees to carbon, with some shaded and some more exposed to light. She used isotopic labeling (carbon atoms with specific numbers of protons as a kind of marking) to track how the carbon traveled between the trees. Simard found that the carbon moved from birch to fir trees, which were

Mycorrhizal fungi often look like plant roots stretching through soil.

connected by a mycorrhizal network, while no carbon was in the cedar trees, which had no mycorrhizal connection. The fir trees took in 6 percent of the birch trees' carbon intake on average, with shaded fir trees getting more carbon than the unshaded ones. Simard's study seems to show that the same kind of transfer that Read simulated in a lab happened in a forest, and fungi were the vehicle for that transfer. When Simard's paper was published in *Nature* magazine, Read wrote a commentary about it and called this fungal network the "wood wide web."

Inside a forest's wood wide web is a diverse network of trees, ranging in size, height, and type and forming a community. The little trees are the youngest, born from seeds of the larger trees. The biggest and oldest in the forest are the mother trees, also called hub trees, which have the most mycorrhizal connections with their immense roots. Simard's research suggests that mother trees communicate and share resources with their community through their fungal connections. They feed the younger trees living in the understory, which are shaded, have fewer leaves, and are unable to produce the same amount of food as the mother tree. Some mother trees send warning signals if insects are attacking them, alerting neighboring trees to initiate their defense systems. Some also send poisons

MAPPING THE WOOD WIDE WEB

In 2019 scientists made a map of the wood wide web by studying trees. Ecologist Thomas Crowther from the university ETH Zurich was the first to map the world's trees, gathering data from governments and scientists who measure and identify trees. Crowther reported in 2015 that close to three trillion trees from twenty-eight thousand different species exist across seventy countries. Stanford University biologist Kabir Peay read this study and asked to collaborate with Crowther to try to map the fungal partnerships between those trees. Knowing the tree species and the fungi or bacteria they partner with, the scientists wrote an algorithm that searched the data to find correlations between the tree type and certain environmental factors, such as temperature and rainfall. Using the results of the algorithm's search, they could fill in where they knew certain kinds of fungi lived on a global map and predict where fungi lived in places without data. Their global map, based on a database of information about certain forests, shows large, interconnected areas in North America, South America, and Europe.

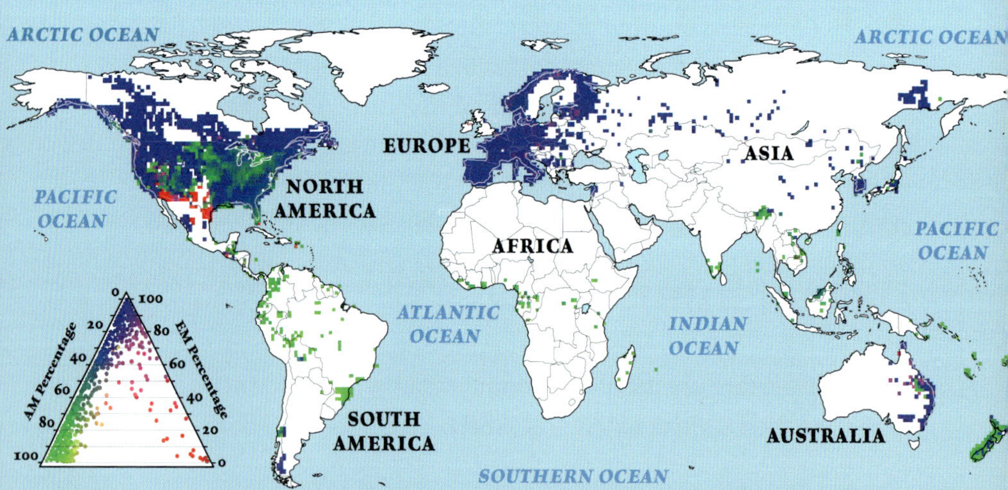

North America has the highest distribution of mixed AM and EM fungi, compared to South America with more AM fungi and Europe with more EM fungi.

through the network if they want to get rid of certain species. Mother trees also seem to detect saplings grown from their seeds and can send more food their way. In one study Simard was involved with, fungi connected a mother tree to forty-seven out of the sixty-seven trees in a plot, showing the tree's importance within a forest network. Simard explained, "I have taken to calling these elders 'Mother Trees' because they appear to be nurturing their young. Mother Trees thus connect the forest through space and time, just like elders connect human families across generations."

One example of this communication and care involves the Douglas fir, ponderosa pine, and foliage-damaging budworms. A study of pairs of fir and pine trees connected by EM fungi showed that when the fir tree's foliage was damaged, either manually by a person or by budworms, it sent carbon and stress signals to its neighboring pine tree through fungi. The pine trees then started their defense responses to help protect them from the insect. Black walnut trees aren't so helpful, though—they use their AM fungal connections to harm neighboring plants. The trees produce a toxin called juglone, which travels along mycorrhizal hyphae and inhibits other connected plants' growth.

While Simard's and others' research into trees' relationships with fungi in forests have good foundations, some researchers think this cooperation may be more complex than we understand. More research and genetic analysis will determine what these relationships are and how they work in forests.

FOREST SHAPERS

Trees may use fungi to communicate and send nutrients in a forest, but the fungi are working on a much bigger scale.

They shape the forest from below, determining how many and which kinds of trees occupy it. Many forests in the north and south worldwide are mostly made up of just a few kinds of trees, while tropical forests along Earth's equator are incredibly diverse. One study estimated that more than 40,000 tropical tree species exist, while only 124 species live in Europe's northern forests.

One difference between the two kinds of forests are the mycorrhizal fungi partnering with the trees. In tropical forests, AM fungi dominate. These fungi aren't selective about the trees they support. That means that any tree growing in the forest could benefit from that partnership, leading to a greater diversity of trees. EM fungi are more common in forests farther from the equator. These fungi can partner only with certain kinds of trees, and they only boost those trees' growth. Any tree not connected to the fungal network has a harder chance of surviving, as it doesn't receive the nutrients and water the other trees do, so EM-dominated forests tend to have just a few tree species.

Whether helping, harming, including, or excluding, mycorrhizal fungi are essential to building and maintaining forest health. And instead of seeing a collection of seemingly separate plants and trees fighting for survival in a crowded space, we can use a mycorrhizal lens to see the community of species woven together by an underground network where messages may travel, food may be shared, and elders may care for their young. It's a radical shift in thought about forest ecology, and researchers are also finding that mushrooms and mycelium can do even more radical things to help the environment—things that could one day save the planet.

CHAPTER 9

PLANET SAVERS, FUTURE BUILDERS

Look closely at adult honeybees, and you might see something strange attached to their bodies—small, round, red-brown insects. They are varroa mites, devastating honeybee parasites that can sweep through a hive over time. These mites' entire life cycle happens within the bee colony. Adult females attach to bees and feed off their haemolymph (their blood) and lay their eggs on bee larvae developing in cells (small chambers made for young in the hive). The hatching mites feed on the larvae's blood, making the bee larvae small and weak. Some bee larvae die within their cells. Surviving bees have a much shorter lifespan than average.

On top of this damage, the mites carry and transmit viruses within the colony. They tap directly into the bees' blood, releasing harmful viruses straight into their bodies. Some evidence shows that the mites also impact the bees' immune systems. The mites hop from bee to bee, spreading their viruses quickly. The bees barely stand a chance when these invaders infect the colony. The viruses can deform and shrivel up bee wings until they are unable to fly, and they affect their abdomens and legs too. The bees can't forage for food, protect the colony, or raise their young. If nothing is done, the whole colony can collapse after a few years.

These mites and the viruses they carry are destroying bee populations around the world. This not only affects the bees but also what the bees do as they feed—pollinate plants. Pollination is essential for flowering plants because insects transfer pollen from one plant to another and allow the plants to grow flowers, fruits, vegetables, and their seeds. This process is critical to world crops. Close to 130 kinds of fruits and vegetables depend on pollination. Without it, we wouldn't have apples, chocolate, nuts, spices, or many other foods we eat. While butterflies and other animals pollinate plants, honeybees are the most important pollinators. They pollinate close to 80 percent of all flowering plants. They are essential to balancing the ecosystem and for agricultural needs. Without bees, we would be in trouble.

Beekeepers have fought back against the mites with chemical control by spraying miticides, pesticides that target mites. But these only kill mites on adult bees, leaving the mites within larvae cells alive. Strips with the chemicals can be placed on the cells to help kill emerging mites, but the chemicals affect hive products, such as honey and wax. The mites have a way to fight back too. They adapt. Their DNA mutates, and soon the chemicals no longer kill them. Some beekeepers switch to organic methods, such as using essential oils, but they are

The hoof fungus, *Fomes femontarius*, is a common polypore mushroom from which amadou derives.

minimally effective. Another method may be key to saving the bees—and it comes from fungi.

World-famous mycologist and author Paul Stamets, who has pioneered many new fungal products and techniques, knew that different fungi have antiviral properties and that bees forage on mycelium. He saw this happening in his own garden, where he kept beehives and grew mushrooms. One day he noticed the bees had moved wood chips to reveal mycelium, and they were sucking on liquid from them. Stamets found this interesting and later tried putting fungi to work to help save the bees from the viruses that were killing them. In 2018 he partnered with Washington State University and the US Department of Agriculture to experiment using his invention—MycoHoney, a sweet feeding liquid for bees that contains mushroom extracts. The extracts came from the polypore mushrooms known to have strong antiviral properties: amadou and reishi mushrooms.

A FUNGIFIED BEE FEEDER

You don't need to be a beekeeper to help save bees from viruses. Soon, anyone will be able to help save the bees! Stamets is developing a special bee feeder to deliver the fungi that help them fight viruses. He calls it the BeeMushroomed Feeder. It contains sugar water with extracts of a fungal solution. When connected to the base, it can be hung up just like a bird feeder. Its base has a maze that is designed to keep out other kinds of bees and wasps, so honeybees get the main benefit of feeding from the fungal solution.

The results of their trials were astounding. Bees fed the MycoHoney lived longer than bees that did not receive it. The deformed wing and Lake Sinai viruses also affected them significantly less. But MycoHoney is still in an experimental phase. Then-Washington State University entomology professor and coauthor of the study Steve Sheppard said, "Our greatest hope is that these extracts have such an impact on viruses that they may help varroa mites become an annoyance for bees, rather than causing huge devastation."

Experiments such as this show that fungi may help us solve many of nature's problems. From keeping pollinators alive to eating plastic, fungi are showing great potential as powerful planet savers. Harnessing their abilities to use on a large scale may be key to protecting our future.

THE POSSIBILITIES OF MYCORESTORATION

Scientists are discovering that different kinds of fungi can do incredible things within the environment. This is mycorestoration—using mushrooms to solve environmental pollution problems and restore balance in nature. Research shows that fungi can be used to filter toxic substances from water, assist in reforestation projects, break down toxic waste sites, and much more. Their studies reveal the promise fungi holds to help clean up our planet.

Mycofiltration uses mycelium to filter water, a technique Stamets pioneered, and it's helping at sites around the world. The River Wandle in South London, Great Britain, became the site of a mycofiltration project in 2014. A group there created mycofilters using a few ingredients layered inside a burlap bag: wet straw, wood chips, and mushroom spawn. They let the bags sit for five weeks so that the mycelium grew throughout. Then they stacked the bags at sites along the river where pollution was entering, such as pipes draining water from an industrial area. As the polluted water flows through the bag, mycelium capture contaminants and prevent them from entering the river. Administrators regularly monitor the microfilters' effectiveness by analyzing water and soil samples.

Another mycofiltration site is on Lake Erie in upstate New York, which had high levels of *E. coli* bacteria in the early 2010s. This bacteria often indicates that animal or sewage waste has contaminated the water, which can introduce many kinds of organisms that cause disease and make the water unsafe for humans. In 2014 the state decided to try mycofiltration using *Stropharia rugosoannulata*, or the garden giant mushroom, known for its ability to remove large amounts of *E. coli* from water. They inoculated wood chips with the mushrooms inside bins that allow water to flow through. They set the bins in spaces where water ran into a stream that fed into the lake. Early findings in 2014 showed that mycofiltration reduced *E. coli* by an average of 40 percent during the summer.

The garden giant mushroom grows well in areas with moist soil and lots of indirect sunlight.

People are using fungi to clean up polluted water in other ways—and clean up burn sites. In Ecuador the Chevron oil company illegally dumped oil into rainforest rivers and soil. CoRenewal, an organization dedicated to ecosystem renewal, is experimenting with fungi to help clean up the massive oil spill. In 2020 the organization also deployed fungi to help restore an area devastated by wildfires in Northern California. The fires destroyed homes, melting plastics and electronics, burning building materials, and releasing metals. Toxic ash covered everything. To help clean the environment, CoRenewal put wattles around the homes to catch any waste the rain washed away. Wattles are long tubes of straw inoculated with fungi. The experiment will show if the fungi can effectively digest toxins from the ash and keep them from entering streams.

PLASTIC-EATING MUSHROOMS

Not much can break down plastic. It piles up in landfills, floats in tiny pieces in the ocean, and can take between twenty and five hundred years to decompose in the environment. It never really disappears, though; it just gets broken down into smaller and smaller pieces. So many products are made using plastic too—from cell phones to disposable bags and cups to many kinds of packaging. Plastic is piling up, harming animals and the environment. But an answer to getting rid of this waste may come from fungi.

Certain kinds of fungi have been found to be able to biodegrade plastic. Researchers in Sydney, Australia, found that *Aspergillus terreus* and *Engyodontium album* can break down polypropylene, a common plastic that makes up about 28 percent of the world's plastic waste. After treating the plastic with UV light or heat, it reduced by 21 percent in thirty days and by 25 to 27 percent in ninety days.

There are other plastic-eating fungi too. A 2023 study of coastal salt marshes where plastic debris collects in Jiang, China, revealed 184 fungal species and fifty-five bacterial strains that break down plastic. That brought the total amount of known plastic-eating fungi and bacteria species to 436. Researchers hope to derive an enzyme from the fungi that could be used to degrade large amounts of plastic.

Using mushrooms that digest toxins in the environment has worked before. They can remove both toxic chemicals and metals from soil and either break them down into less harmful substances, such as carbon and oxygen, or concentrate them within their fruiting bodies. In 1998 Stamets tested the effect of oyster mushrooms on oil-contaminated soil at the maintenance yard of the Washington State Department of Transportation. He used four piles of contaminated soil and inoculated one with the fungus, two with bacterial treatments, and left one untreated as a control. After eight weeks, the pile with the fungus was filled with oyster mushrooms and smelled clean, while the others still smelled of fuel. Researchers tested the soil, and its total petroleum hydrocarbons (chemicals that come from crude oil) had dropped from 20,000 parts per million (ppm) to 200 ppm, making it safe to use for highway landscaping.

Mycoforestry taps into the potential for mushrooms to restore forests and protect against deforestation. Adding mycorrhizal fungi to newly planted trees in forests that have been destroyed can greatly improve their ability to grow and thrive, boosting reforestation efforts. Choosing native, beneficial fungi for the types of trees planted is essential. Stamets and his team are testing mycoforestry in a plot of land he owns on Cortes Island in British Columbia, Canada, that the previous owner clear-cut. They divided the area into four test plots and planted thirty-five thousand native Douglas fir and cedar saplings in them. They dipped half of the saplings' root balls in a mixture containing spores before planting them. The other saplings did not receive this treatment before being planted. In addition, the team spread wood chip mulch around the trunks of half of the treated and untreated saplings. They are tracking data from trees in each of the plots to see the effects of the added mushrooms and wood chip mulch. After ten months, the team recorded that the treated trees were already 8 percent taller and 7 percent bigger than the untreated trees. Over many years, their collected data will show what inoculating saplings with spores can do to help reforestation efforts.

While these and other fungal solutions are very promising, they are still being tested and have some limitations, including the amount of time they take to effectively remove toxins from the environment. It will take more research to determine how we can harness their power to restore the environment at a larger scale.

FUTURISTIC MACHINES AND PRODUCTS

Fungi can do more than attack and destroy pollutants—they can also build new things people need and want. Innovators are experimenting with ways to create futuristic machines and products with fungi.

One experimenter runs a laboratory in Bristol, England: Professor Andy Adamatzky, head of the Unconventional Computing Laboratory at the University of the West of England. His research focuses on using mycelial connections and their ability to transmit signals for a very unconventional purpose—to create experimental laboratory computing devices. Using living material to make computers of the future is called wet computing. Adamatzky believes, "The computers of 2100 [and beyond] will be made of living and chemical systems. They will either be purely 'wet computers' or hybrid computers where wetware, hardware, and software work together harmoniously." He records electrical activity within oyster, ghost, bracket, enoki, split gill, and caterpillar fungi. By monitoring fungi with electrodes, he's found that they transmit spikes of electrical energy through their mycelium. These spikes may transmit information. Evidence supports this theory: The spikes change when the fungi are stimulated mechanically, chemically, and optically. Adamatzky aims to understand this communication better and develop and prototype computing devices made with fungi.

Additionally, Adamatzky is experimenting with using fungi in architecture. His work centers on creating "intelligent buildings" with fungal sensors integrated into their structure and the ability to build themselves and self-repair any damage. He's part of a consortium (association) of architects, computer scientists, biophysicists, mycologists, and industry experts in mycelium-based technologies. Together they are researching how fungi can be used to make these intelligent structures with mycelial computers built into their walls.

Other innovators look at fungal structures as a better ecological alternative to traditional building materials. One example is the Hy-Fi, a structure developed by the architecture firm the Living. Collaborating with Ecovative, a company that uses mycelium to make packaging materials, they created bricks from cornstalks and mycelium. The bricks take five days to grow and are lightweight and durable when completed. The team tested the bricks' strength by simulating weathering at an accelerated rate and found that they remained highly durable.

COMPOSTABLE FUNGI PACKAGING

The packaging that Ecovative is making could change packaging forever. Traditional packaging is made from plastic and Styrofoam, materials that end up in landfills and do not biodegrade. Ecovative's packaging is fully compostable because it's made by growing mycelium with agricultural matter, such as hemp or cornstalks. The company grows them in molds and then heat-treats the material to stop growth. They call this packaging Mushroom Packaging (or MycoComposite). Other companies are starting to adopt this packaging alternative, which is sustainable and good for the environment.

The Hy-Fi consisted of ten thousand bricks. The team built it over the course of summer in 2014.

After the tests, they used the bricks to build a 40-foot-tall (12 m) tower called the Hy-Fi to show how this organically grown building material could one day become a replacement for current more toxic materials. The project won the 2014 Young Architects Program competition at the Museum of Modern Art in New York City.

Fashion-forward innovators are using fungi to produce clothing. So far they've made a kind of vegan leather combining mycelium and a substrate such as cellulose (a structural part of plant cell walls). This alternative to animal skin is sustainable and durable, and the Stella McCartney and Hermès fashion houses are already using it in their collections. Some scientists are researching ways to use fungi in a self-healing kind of fabric too. If you punch a hole in it, it can regrow!

MUSHROOMS ON MARS

While mushrooms are being used in many ways on Earth, they may soon travel through space to perform another important job—building a colony on Mars. NASA is preparing to send astronauts to Mars in the 2030s, and when they arrive, they will need somewhere to live and work on the red planet. But carrying building materials millions of miles from Earth would add weight to the spacecraft and cost fuel energy. That's why scientists at NASA's Ames Research Center are looking for a lighter alternative. Fungi may be just the solution for structures on the moon, Mars, and other possible sites in space.

The team is in the early stages of researching a way to grow habitats in space using lightweight frames containing mushroom spores. They envision a three-layered dome structure. The outer layer would consist of frozen water, found on both Mars and the moon, and would protect the habitat from the sun's radiation. It could trickle water onto the second layer underneath, which would contain cyanobacteria. This organism uses water and sunlight that shines through the ice to photosynthesize, producing oxygen for astronauts and food for fungi below. The inner layer would contain the fungi, whose mycelium would grow to form an enclosed structure. Engineers could then treat the mycelium with heat to halt its growth and make the layer more stable.

The laboratory is also looking at other ways fungi could be used on the colony—for lighting (bioluminescence), to filter water, regulate humidity, and even self-repair its structures. Through their experiments, the scientists may find a solution for astronauts' habitat needs using fungi as their building material and inspiration.

OUR FUNGI-FILLED FUTURE

How will fungi shape our world (and maybe even Mars)? Their uses are diverse and still being discovered—from healing our bodies and minds to restoring our planet and building a more ecologically mindful world. And all this is happening from just about 10 percent of the fungi that already exist in our world. What will we discover in the other 90 percent of fungal species? These connectors of life, our fungal partners, may provide the solutions we need for our future survival. By exploring and discovering our planet's fungi, we may find possibilities that are currently unimaginable, such as cures for currently uncurable diseases, methods for making toxic waste sites disappear, or ways to construct buildings that can grow and think for themselves. Fungi will continue to shape and change our world far into the future—destroying, healing, feeding, connecting, and possibly pushing us toward a more sustainable existence on Earth.

ARE YOU A MYCOPHILE?

Lots of people fall in love with fungi—they are just so interesting and mysterious to find and study. There are many amateur mycologists and mycophiles all over the world. Here are a few ways to connect with them, share your knowledge, and learn about different kinds of fungi:

1. Join a mycological society in your area. Fees are often low, and education and connection are what draw people to join. Guest mycologists give lectures, and members go out on forays to find mushrooms in the wild. Members can also attend cooking classes and workshops, and they have a group to share their fungal findings with.

2. Get a reputable guidebook for mushroom identification. Find one specific to your region. And bring someone experienced in mushroom identification on any forays you take.

3. Join online communities through citizen science apps, such as iNaturalist. If you upload pictures of fungi you find, the app can help you identify them, and community members can comment on their identity too. The app also shares members' findings with scientific data repositories, letting nonscientists contribute to biodiversity research.

4. Be part of the Fungal Diversity Survey to document and protect fungi. It connects with iNaturalist and allows members to start or join different projects studying fungi. The Fungal Diversity Database is one of the survey's programs on iNaturalist that collects data about fungi from citizen scientists.

5. Go hiking to find places where fungi grow. Keep a journal of what you find and where the fungi are located. Become familiar with fungi habitats in your area. Try to identify what you see.

6. Grow some mushrooms to understand them better and have some delicious additions to your meals. Different companies sell mushroom-growing kits you can try for both indoor and outdoor mushroom crops. Small indoor kits just need water to begin growing. Outdoor kits are more difficult, usually involving a log or other kind of growth medium. With these kits, you can grow oyster, lion's mane, shiitake, and other delicious mushrooms.

ACKNOWLEDGMENTS

I'd like to thank the following contributors for their expertise and advice while developing this book:

- Dr. Bryn Dentinger, associate professor and curator of mycology, School of Biological Sciences & Natural History Museum of Utah, University of Utah
- Dr. Jessie Uehling, assistant professor, Department of Botany and Plant Pathology, Oregon State University; mycologist for the Oregon Psilocybin Advisory Board
- Dr. Natalie Gukasyan, assistant professor, Columbia University Medical Center/New York State Psychiatric Institute; affiliate investigator, Johns Hopkins Center for Psychedelic and Consciousness Research
- Professor Andrew Adamatzky, Unconventional Computing Laboratory; University of the West of England, Bristol, United Kingdom
- Peter Martignacco, president, Minnesota Mycological Society (125 Years of Citizen Science)
- Ron Spinosa, mushroom identifier, Minnesota Mycological Society
- Steve Unverzagt, amateur mycologist and truffle hunter; member of the Minnesota Mycological Society and the North American Truffle Growers Association

GLOSSARY

agaric: mushroom with gills

bioluminescent: the emission of light from organisms due to an internal chemical reaction

bolete fungi: fungi with tubes, also called polypores

chitin: a material found in the cell walls of fungi and the exoskeletons of insects, spiders, and crustaceans

clinical trial: a scientifically controlled study of the safety and effectiveness of a therapy, drug, or vaccine using consenting human subjects, with four phases. Phase I, to see if a treatment is safe for humans, includes fifteen to fifty patients. Phase II, to see if a treatment works, includes fewer than one hundred patients. Phase III includes hundreds to thousands of patients. It uses a control and study group to see if the new treatment is better than standard treatments. Phase IV occurs after the FDA has approved the treatment's use to continue studying the treatment's side effects.

digestive enzymes: proteins that break down food so that an organism can digest it

fermentation: the chemical process liquid undergoes when it contains actively growing microorganisms

fruiting body: mushroom; reproductive structure of fungi

gleba: a sticky, slimy mass that contains fungal spores

guttation: exuding liquid from an uninjured surface of a fungi or plant

heterotrophic organisms: organisms that cannot produce their own food and must find it in their environment

hypha: individual fungal cells that grow from end to end to form long chains of cells

lichen: organisms made up of an alga or a cyanobacterium and a fungus growing in symbiotic association on a solid surface

microorganism: an organism that is microscopic in size

mold: a superficial often woolly growth produced especially on damp or decaying organic matter or on living organisms by a fungus

mushroom: the fruiting body, or reproductive structure of fungi

mycelia: a network of fungal cells, or hyphae

mycobiome: the fungal community living inside or on an organism

mycology: the study of fungi

mycoparasitism: when an organism lives off a fungi

mycorrhizal: the symbiotic state of mycelia that form on tree roots and other plants

psilocybin: a hallucinogenic chemical produced by certain fungi

sporangiophore: special hyphae that grow into the air to shoot out spores

spore: the reproductive cell of fungi used to spread fungi to new environments

substrate: the material fungi grow in, such as hay, sawdust, manure, or wood

symbiosis: a cooperative living association between two dissimilar organisms

tooth fungi: fungi with mushrooms that have spines

truffle hound: a dog trained to find truffles in the ground

yeast: single-celled fungi that live in colonies

SOURCE NOTES

5 "like mycelium of fungus": Francis M. Hueber, "Rotted Wood—Alga—Fungus: The History and Life of Prototaxites Dawson 1859," *Review of Palaeobotany and Palynology* 116 (August 2001): 126, https://www.sciencedirect.com/science/article/abs/pii/S0034666701000586.

14 "Whetstone wanted to . . . of their hunger.": Peter Martignacco, interview with the author, June 22, 2023.

28 "My studies started . . . or Ling Zhi).": Jessie Uehling, interview with the author, July 29, 2023.

29 "We had a . . . in the tropics!": Uehling.

29 "I grew up . . . exposed me to.": Uehling.

29 "AP sciences courses . . . level science classes": Uehling.

29 "one of my . . . call the mycofam": Uehling.

29 "try to get . . . of career development.": Uehling.

38 "On the inside . . . in the dark.": Benjamin Gale to Silas Deane, November 9, 1775, Naval History and Heritage Command, https://www.history.navy.mil/research/library/online-reading-room/title-list-alphabetically/s/submarine-turtle-naval-documents.html#item1.

51 "This is very . . . the food industry.": "'Sophisticated': Ancient Faeces Shows Humans Enjoyed Beer and Blue Cheese 2,700 Years Ago," *Guardian* (US edition), October 13, 2021, https://www.theguardian.com/science/2021/oct/14/sophisticated-ancient-faeces-shows-humans-enjoyed-beer-and-blue-cheese-2700-years-ago.

60 "That Claudius was . . . was extravagantly fond.": R. Gordon Wasson, *Botanical Museum Leaflets*, Harvard University 23, no. 3 (April 7, 1972): 118, https://archive.org/details/biostor-160863.

61 "It was then . . . time to kill.": Wasson, 120.

62 "ICG has shown . . . saves people's lives.": Bei Wang et al., "Identification of Indocyanine Green as a STT3B Inhibitor Against Mushroom α-Amanitin Cytotoxicity," *Nature Communications* 14, no. 2241 (2023), https://doi.org/10.1038/s41467-023-37714-3.

72 “The mushroom helps . . . to the brain.”: Audrey Henson, “Treating Dementia in Japan: How a Mushroom and a Community Work Together,” Pulitzer Center, October 31, 2019, https://pulitzercenter.org/stories/treating-dementia-japan-how-mushroom-and-community-work-together.

72 “Kouka, paired with . . . taking the [Kouka].”: Masaru Takahashi, quoted in Henson.

84–85 “My world just . . . and dark future.”: “State of Mind: Psilocybin Therapy,” WebMD video, 0:39, January 4, 2022, https://www.webmd.com/mental-health/story/psychedelic-psilocybin-study-depression.

85 “Suddenly, I wasn’t . . . last that long.”: Paul Frysh, “One Man’s Psychedelic Journey to Confront His Cancer,” WebMD, January 4, 2022, https://www.webmd.com/mental-health/story/psychedelic-psilocybin-study-depression.

85 “I don’t have . . . states of mind.”: Frysh.

87 “It seems that . . . and at peace.”: Frysh.

90 “used to treat . . . a week after.”: C. Van Court et al., “Diversity, Biology, and History of Psilocybin-Containing Fungi: Suggestions for Research and Technological Development,” *Fungal Biology* 126, no. 4 (2022), https://www.sciencedirect.com/science/article/pii/S1878614622000095.

92 “peer reviewed, western . . . recently eating disorders.”: Uehling, interview.

93 “On a biological . . . many other functions.”: Natalie Gukasyan, interview with the author, July 25, 2023.

93–94 “One level up . . . of a mystery.”: Gukasyan.

94 “I lost my . . . to the world.”: Uehling, interview.

94 “a special window . . . change those patterns.”: Gukasyan.

95 “It probably will . . . of that research.”: Gukasyan.

95–96 “Serious risks can . . . issue like psychosis.”: Gukasyan.

96 “He taught me . . . with fruit flies.”: Gukasyan.

96–97 “In short we . . . quality of life.”: Gukasyan.

97 “interesting research papers . . . the right time.”: Gukasyan.

97 “I did my . . . learning from them.”: Gukasyan.

97 “But it’s exhilarating . . . is very rewarding.”: Gukasyan.

100 “’Tis whiter than . . . be not Tragedy—”: Emily Dickinson, “’Tis Whiter Than an Indian Pipe—” Morgan Library & Museum, accessed December 15, 2024, https://www.themorgan.org/exhibitions/online/emily-dickinson/23.

105 “wood wide web”: Merlin Sheldrake, *Entangled Life* (Random House, 2020), 169.

107 “I have taken . . . families across generations.”: S. W. Simard, “The Mother Tree,” in Anna Sophie Springer and Etienne Turpin, eds., *The Word for World Is Still Forest* (K. Verlag and the Haus der Kulturen), 2017, Mother Tree Project, accessed December 15, 2024, https://mothertreeproject.org/wp-content/uploads/2020/01/the-mother-tree_the_word_for_world_is_still_forest.pdf.

112 “Our greatest hope . . . causing huge devastation.”: Communications staff, “Fungus Provides Powerful Medicine in Fighting Honeybee Viruses,” Washington State University Insider, October 4, 2018, https://news.wsu.edu/news/2018/10/04/fungus-provides-powerful-medicine-fighting-honey-bee-viruses.

117 “The computers of . . . work together harmoniously.”: Andy Adamatzky, interview with the author, March 11, 2023.

SELECTED BIBLIOGRAPHY

Adamatzky, Andrew. "Language of Fungi Derived from Their Electrical Spiking Activity." *Royal Society Open Science* 9, no. 4 (April 2022). https://doi.org/10.1098/rsos.211926.

Bonfante, Paola, and Andrea Genre. "Mechanisms Underlying Beneficial Plant–Fungus Interactions in Mycorrhizal Symbiosis." *Nature Communications* 1, no. 48 (2010). https://doi.org/10.1038/ncomms1046.

Fantastic Fungi. Directed by Louie Schwartzberg. Produced by Louie Schwartzberg, Elease Lui, and Lyn Lear. Moving Art Studio, 2019.

Finlay, R. D., and D. J. Read. "The Structure and Function of the Vegetative Mycelium of Ectomycorrhizal Plants. *New Phytologist* 103, no. 1 (1986): 143–156. https://doi.org/10.1111/j.1469-8137.1986.tb00603.x.

John's Hopkins Medicine, Psychedelics Research and Psilocybin. Accessed December 15, 2024. https://www.hopkinsmedicine.org/psychiatry/research/psychedelics-research.

Peintner, Ursula, R. Pöder, and Thomas Pümpel. "The Iceman's Fungi." *Mycological Research* 102, no. 10 (October 1998): 1153–1162. https://doi.org/10.1017/S0953756298006546.

Sheldrake, Merlin. *Entangled Life*. Random House, 2020.

Song, Yuan Yuan, Suzanne W. Simard, Allan Carroll, William W. Mohn, and Ren Sen Zeng. "Defoliation of Interior Douglas-Fir Elicits Carbon Transfer and Stress Signalling to Ponderosa Pine Neighbors Through Ectomycorrhizal Networks." *Scientific Reports* 5 (2015): 8495. https://doi.org/10.1038/srep08495.

Stamets, Paul, ed. *Fantastic Fungi*. Earth Aware, 2019.

Stamets, Paul. *Mycelium Running: How Mushrooms Can Help Save the World*. Ten Speed, 2005.

Stamets Paul E., Nicholas L. Naeger, Jay D. Evans et al. "Extracts of Polypore Mushroom Mycelia Reduce Viruses in Honey Bees." *Scientific Reports* 8 (October 2018): 13936. https://doi.org/10.1038/s41598-018-32194-8.

Tom Volk's Fungi, Department of Biology, University of Wisconsin–LaCrosse. Accessed December 15, 2024. https://botit.botany.wisc.edu/toms_fungi/.

Van Court, R. C., M. S. Wiseman, K. W. Meyer et al. "Diversity, Biology, and History of Psilocybin-Containing Fungi: Suggestions for Research and Technological Development." *Fungal Biology* 126, no. 4 (April 2022): 308–319. https://www.sciencedirect.com/science/article/pii/S1878614622000095.

FURTHER RESOURCES

Fungal Diversity Survey
https://fundis.org
This nonprofit focuses on North America's fungal biodiversity and conservation by providing ways citizen scientists can share their fungal findings.

iNaturalist
https://www.inaturalist.org
Join other citizen scientists as they observe nature, upload their pictures to share with the iNaturalist community, and then discuss their findings.

Minnesota Mycological Society
https://minnesotamycologicalsociety.org
This educational organization exists to help members improve their mushroom identification skills, build the mycological collection at the University of Minnesota, educate the public about fungi, and assist in mushroom identification.

MycoBank
https://www.mycobank.org
This online database documents fungi names and types.

National Audubon Society. *Field Guide to Mushrooms: North America*. Alfred A. Knopf, 2000.
This mushroom identification field guide has photographs and information about many species of fungi.

North American Mycological Association
https://namyco.org
This organization of professional and amateur mycologists serves over ninety affiliated mycological societies in the United States, Canada, and Mexico.

Stamets, Paul. "6 Ways Mushrooms Can Save the World." TED Talk, March 2008. https://www.ted.com/talks/paul_stamets_6_ways_mushrooms_can_save_the_world?subtitle=en.
This TED Talk by world-famous mycologist Paul Stamets describes ways that mushrooms can help people and our planet.

INDEX

ABOUT THE AUTHOR

Karen Latchana Kenney is an Indian-Irish author and editor, born near the equator in Guyana, and raised far north in Minnesota. She writes both fiction and nonfiction stories about scientific wonders and discoveries, immigrant and biracial experiences, momentous historical events, and civil rights struggles. Her books have received several starred reviews and have been named a 2023 Mathical Book Prize Honor book and a YALSA Quick Pick for Reluctant Readers. She lives in Minnesota with her designer-musician husband and mathematician–robot-building son, where they explore all the wild places they can find and search for fungi wherever they go.

PHOTO ACKNOWLEDGMENTS

Image Credits: Jolanda Aalbers/Shutterstock, p. 1; Oleg Marchak/Getty Images, pp. 2, 131; Ed Reschke/Getty Images, pp. 2, 3, 66, 126, 127, 132, 133; Minh Hoang Cong / 500px/Getty Images, pp. 2, 130 (bottom); John Quixley - Australia/Alamy, pp. 3, 25, 121, 125; Wikimedia Commons PD, pp. 6, 88, 111; LukaSkywalker/Shutterstock, p. 12; zombiu26/Shutterstock, p. 17; Ruben Duro/Science Source, p. 23; Anne Powell/Shutterstock, p. 26; Alan Mirza/ Shutterstock, p. 27; Courtesy of Jessie Uehling, p. 28; Dan Molter/Wikimedia Commons CC BY-SA 3.0, p. 30; Emanuele Biggi/naturepl.com, p. 31; Ionescu Bogdan Cristian/Alamy, p. 32; Enya Roseli/Shutterstock, p. 33; mauribo/ Getty Images, p. 35; IgorCheri/Shutterstock, p. 36; Library of Congress, p. 36; Cassius V. Stevani/IQ-USP, Brazil, p. 37; AlbyDeTweede/Getty Images, p. 39; Connie Pinson/Getty Images, p. 40; DP Wildlife Fungi/Alamy, p. 41; Dr Morley Read/Science Source, p. 42; AP Photo/Andrew Medichini, p. 45; Georg Berg/Alamy, p. 49; Stewart Innes/Alamy, p. 55; blickwinkel/Alamy, p. 58; Jaroslav Machacek/Shutterstock, p. 60; © Izawa Masana/Minden Pictures, p. 65; Inga spence/Alamy, p. 68; Knn Linku/Shutterstock, p. 71; Vlad Imir/ Shutterstock, p. 73; Colin Hunter/Alamy, p. 75; Science Photo Library/Alamy, p. 81; 24K-Production/Alamy, p. 86; Johns Hopkins Center for Psychedelic and Consciousness Research, p. 93; Dr. Natalie Gukasyan , p. 96; AP Photo/ Andrew Selsky, p. 98; Lindsay Kaulback/Shutterstock, p. 99; Nigel Cattlin/ Alamy, p. 105; Ann B./Wikimedia Commons (CC BY-SA 3.0), p. 115; Inhabitat/ flickr (CC BY-NC-ND 2.0), p. 119; David Clapp/Getty Images, pp. 121, 123 (left); iStockphoto/Getty Images, pp. 128–129. Design Elements: krungchingpixs/ Shutterstock; James Aloysius Mahan V/Shutterstock; luchschenF/ Shutterstock; Protasov AN/Shutterstock; Jaroslav Machacek/Shutterstock.

Cover: Protasov AN/Shutterstock; Fotorina/Shutterstock; Mindhive/ Shutterstock; krungchingpixs/Shutterstock.